Excel for Windows® 95 Essentials

Project 1	**Getting Started with Excel for Windows 95** Creating a List of Office Expenses 3
Project 2	**Building a Spreadsheet** Creating an Office Expense Budget 33
Project 3	**Improving the Appearance of a Worksheet** Formatting a Budget 63
Project 4	**Calculating with Functions** Projecting Office Expenses 87
Project 5	**Using Charts and Maps** Charting Income 111
Project 6	**Managing Data** Creating an Address Database 139
Project 7	**Using Excel with Other Programs** Integrating Applications 159
	Appendix A Working with Windows 95 177
	Index 187

Suzanne Weixel
Adrienne Seymour, M.Ed.

Excel for Windows 95 Essentials

Copyright © 1996 by Que ® Education & Training

All rights reserved. Printed in the United States of America. No part of this book may be used or reproduced in any form or by any means, or stored in a database or retrieval system, without prior written permission of the publisher except in the case of brief quotations embodied in critical articles and reviews. Making copies of any part of this book for any purpose other than your own personal use is a violation of United States copyright laws. For information, address Que Education and Training, Macmillan Computer Publishing, 201 W. 103rd Street, Indianapolis, IN 46290.

Library of Congress Catalog No.: 95-74865

ISBN: 1-57576-002-9

This book is sold *as is*, without warranty of any kind, either express or implied, respecting the contents of this book, including but not limited to implied warranties for the book's quality, performance, merchantability, or fitness for any particular purpose. Neither Que Corporation nor its dealers or distributors shall be liable to the purchaser or any other person or entity with respect to any liability, loss, or damage caused or alleged to be caused directly or indirectly by this book.

99 98 97 96   4 3 2 1

Interpretation of the printing code: the rightmost double-digit number is the year of the book's printing; the rightmost single-digit number, the number of the book's printing. For example, a printing code of 96-1 shows that the first printing of the book occurred in 1996.

Screens reproduced in this book were created using Collage Plus from Inner Media, Inc., Hollis, NH.

President and Publisher: David P. Ewing

Associate Publisher: Chris Katsaropoulos

Publishing Director: Charles O. Stewart III

Product Marketing Manager: Susan J. Dollman

Acquisitions Editors: Rob Tidrow
                     Diane E. Beausoleil

Managing Editor: Jenny Watson

Production Editor: Sally A. Yuska

Cover Designer: Ann Jones

Book Designer: Gary Adair

Production Team: Mary Ann Abramson, Michael Brumitt, Charlotte Clapp, Terrie Deemer, Jason Hand, Kevin Laseau, Paula Lowell, Nancy C. Price, Brian-Kent Proffitt, Bobbi Satterfield, Mark Walchle

Trademark Acknowledgments

All terms mentioned in this book that are known to be trademarks or service marks have been appropriately capitalized. Que Education and Training cannot attest to the accuracy of this information. Use of a term in this book should not be regarded as affecting the validity of any trademark or service mark.

Microsoft and Windows are registered trademarks of Microsoft Corporation.

Developed by Tim Huddleston

Technical review by Kurt B. Barthelmess

Composed in *Stone Serif* and *MCPdigital* by Que Corporation

Project 1

Getting Started with Excel

Creating a List of Office Expenses

In this project, you learn how to
- Start Excel
- Learn Parts of the Excel Screen
- Get Help
- Move around the Worksheet
- Enter Data
- Save a Worksheet
- Print a Worksheet
- Exit Excel

Project 1   Getting Started with Excel

Why Would I Do This?

Computer spreadsheet software is the application software that started the personal computer revolution. That's because spreadsheet software, such as Microsoft Excel, is a versatile tool that can be used for both personal and business use. As you work through the projects in this book, you will find that spreadsheet technology enables you to calculate and display your business applications easily and flexibly. Thus, spreadsheets aid your thought processes and save you time.

Basically, spreadsheet software turns your computer into a business analysis tool. Many people compare spreadsheets to pocket calculators, but spreadsheets have capabilities that are many times more powerful than even the most high-tech calculator. At the most basic level, Excel enables you to decide what data you want to see and how it will be displayed—something no pocket calculator can duplicate. You will explore these features of Excel first.

Default
The settings that a program uses unless you specify another setting. For example, in Excel, the default column width is 8.43 characters.

In this project, you begin to learn how spreadsheets work and what you can do with them by starting the software and taking a tour of the Microsoft Excel screen. You also get a taste of how spreadsheets can help you by creating a list of personal expenses. After you create the list, you learn how to save your work and print it.

Lesson 1: Starting Excel

Worksheet
One page of your work in an Excel for Windows 95 workbook.

The first thing you need to know about Excel is how to start the software. You must be up and running in Windows 95 before you can start Excel. If you are not familiar with Windows 95 or using the mouse, see Appendix A, "Working with Windows 95," at the end of this book.

Workbook
An Excel file that contains single or multiple worksheets.

When you first start Excel, the program displays a blank *workbook* titled `Book1`, which displays a blank *worksheet*, titled `Sheet1`. In Project 2, you learn to create a new worksheet and work on an existing worksheet.

In this lesson, you use the blank *default* worksheet supplied by Excel. Try starting Excel now.

To Start Excel

❶ Turn on your computer and monitor.

The computer loads Windows 95, and the Windows Desktop should appear on your screen, as shown in Figure 1.1. (Your screen may appear slightly different, depending on how Windows is set up on your computer.) When you see the Windows Desktop, you are ready to start Excel for Windows 95.

Lesson 1: Starting Excel   E–5

Figure 1.1
The Windows 95 Desktop.

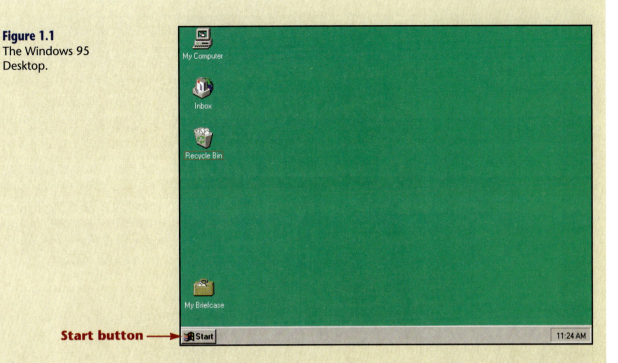

Start button

② **Click the Start button on the taskbar (refer to Figure 1.1).**

The Start menu opens on the desktop (see Figure 1.2). From the Start menu, you can start programs and open documents, get help, find files or folders, change settings, and shut down Windows 95. For more information on using the Start menu or the taskbar, see Appendix A, "Working With Windows 95," at the end of this book.

Figure 1.2
When you move the mouse pointer to the **P**rograms item on the Start menu, a nested menu of installed programs appears.

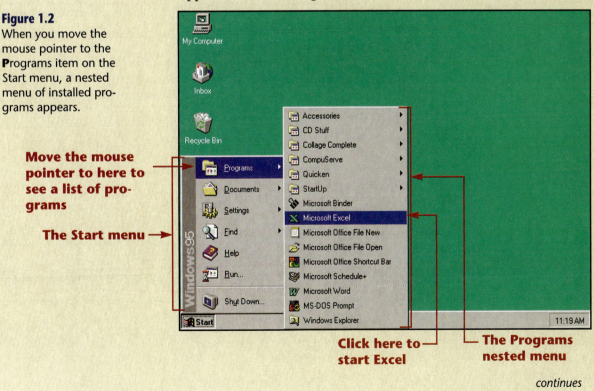

Move the mouse pointer to here to see a list of programs

The Start menu

Click here to start Excel

The Programs nested menu

continues

To Start Excel (continued)

Nested menu
A submenu of options that appears when you choose some menu items in Windows 95. A small, right-pointing arrowhead appears to the right of menu items that have nested menus.

3 **Move the mouse pointer to the Programs item at the top of the Start menu.**

A *nested menu*, listing the programs installed on your computer, appears on the desktop to the right of the Start menu, as shown in Figure 1.2.

> **If you have problems...**
>
> Because you can customize Windows 95, your desktop may look different from the one shown in the illustrations in this book. Your Programs menu may be different from the menu illustrated in this book, depending on the programs you have installed on your computer.

4 **Click Microsoft Excel in the Programs nested menu.**

Excel starts, and the Excel screen appears with the default workbook and worksheet displayed, as shown in Figure 1.3. Now you can begin using Excel.

Figure 1.3
The Excel default workbook and worksheet.

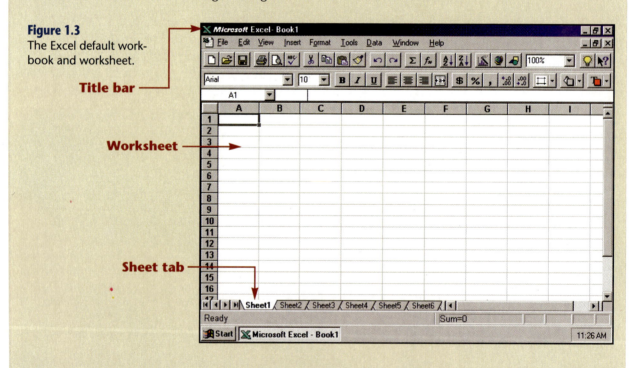

Keep this workbook open to use in the next lesson.

Lesson 2: Learning Parts of the Excel Screen

With Excel for Windows 95 up and running on your computer, it's time to learn about the Excel screen. You may recognize some of the elements from other Windows programs, such as the minimize and maximize buttons, the control-menu box, scroll bars, title bar, menu bar, and so on. Other elements of the screen are features of Excel that will help you complete your work quickly and efficiently. The formula line, sheet tabs, and toolbars are convenient tools that you will use in most of the projects throughout this book.

Again, for more information on the common elements of the Windows screen, see Appendix A, "Working with Windows 95," at the end of this book.

To get to know the elements of the Excel screen, take a look at Figure 1.4.

Now try finding your way around the Excel screen on your computer. (If you need help, see Figure 1.4.)

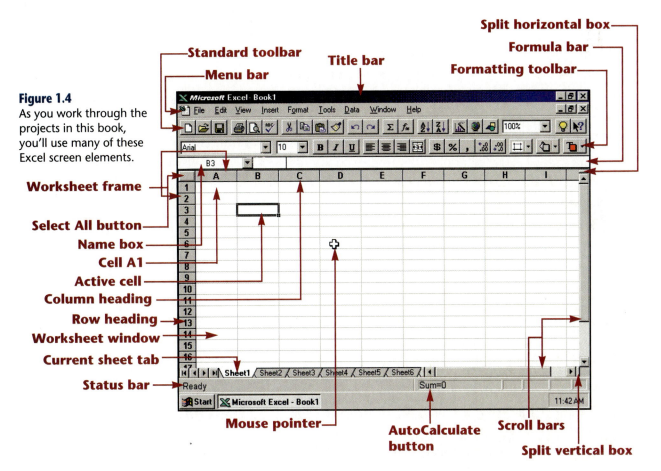

Figure 1.4
As you work through the projects in this book, you'll use many of these Excel screen elements.

Project 1   Getting Started with Excel

To Learn Parts of the Excel Screen

① Using the mouse, click File on the menu bar.

This opens the File menu. Notice that Excel menus appear the same as menus in any Windows program. In Excel, you can open menus and choose commands to perform actions. You can cancel a menu by clicking the menu name again, by clicking anywhere in the window outside of the menu, or by pressing Esc twice.

② Click the word File again to cancel, or close, the menu.

③ Move the mouse pointer to the workbook window's title bar.

The title bar contains the names of the program and the workbook, as well as other Window 95 elements such as the maximize, minimize, and close buttons.

④ Move the mouse pointer to any cell of the worksheet, and then click the left mouse button.

An outline appears around the *cell* to indicate that the cell is the *current cell*, or *active cell*. The cell's *address*—such as A1 or B1—appears in the *name box* to let you know which cell is selected. The selected cell is where any typing or new action will take place.

⑤ Move the mouse pointer around the edges of the selected cell.

Notice that the mouse pointer changes from a white plus sign to an arrow when you are near the cell boundary. In later projects, you will see that as you perform different actions on the selected cell, the mouse pointer assumes different shapes.

⑥ Click the column heading for column A.

The entire column becomes selected, or highlighted, except for cell A1, which remains normal. You can select any column or row by clicking the column letter or row number in the *worksheet frame*. You select a column or row to perform an action—such as copying or deleting—on the information in the selected area.

 ⑦ Move the mouse pointer to the Bold button on the Formatting toolbar.

The fourth line of the Excel screen is the *Formatting toolbar*. Buttons on the toolbars are small pictures that represent actions you can perform—generally, the most common actions you perform or menu commands you choose when using Excel. If you click a button only once, you trigger the action that the button represents. Remember, you need only single-click the toolbar buttons, not double-click.

 To find out what any button does, position the mouse pointer over the button and leave it there for a moment. In a second or two, a ToolTip appears, containing a description of that button.

Lesson 2: Learning Parts of the Excel Screen

If you have problems...

If the ToolTips don't appear, open the **V**iew menu and choose **T**oolbars. The Toolbars dialog box appears. In the dialog box, click the **S**how ToolTips check box, choose OK, and then try again.

Jargon Watch

Key terms are defined for you throughout this book when they are first used. When a number of computer terms are introduced in the same lesson, you will see a Jargon Watch box like this one to help take some of the mystery out of the words.

In this lesson, you have had to wade through a lot of computer jargon. Because you have just been introduced to a number of spreadsheet basics, Table 1.1 lists and describes all the screen elements in Figure 1.4 and defines all the key terms used in this lesson.

Table 1.1   Parts of the Excel Screen

Element	Description
Active cell	The highlighted cell where the next action you take, such as typing or formatting, happens.
Address	Describes which column and row intersect to form the cell; for example, A1 is the address for the first cell in the first column (column A) and the first row (row 1).
AutoCalculate	Displays the sum of the contents of the currently selected range of cells. If you want to change the AutoCalculate function to something other than SUM, move the mouse pointer to the AutoCalculate button, click the right mouse button and choose from the list.
Cell	The intersection of a column and a row.
Cell A1	The first or topmost cell in a worksheet.
Cell contents	The contents of the active cell.
Column heading	Lettered A through Z, then AA through AZ, and so on through IV, up to 256 columns.
Formatting toolbar	Represents various shortcuts to the Format menu commands, such as Font, Bold, Italic, Underline, Alignment, Numeric display, and so on, in button form.
Formula bar	Displays the address and contents of the current, or selected, cell.
Menu bar	Contains common menu names that, when activated, display a list of related commands; the **E**dit menu, for example, contains commands such as Cu**t**, **C**opy, **P**aste, and Cle**a**r.
Mouse pointer	Selects items and positions the insertion point (cursor).

continues

Project 1 Getting Started with Excel

Table 1.1 Continued

Element	Description
Name box	Displays the cell address of the current or selected cell, or a named range.
Row heading	Numbered 1 through 16,384.
Scroll bars	Enable you to move the worksheet window vertically and horizontally so that you can see other parts of the worksheet.
Sheet tab	Displays tabs representing each sheet in the workbook. Click a sheet tab to quickly move to that sheet.
Select All button	Selects all cells in the current worksheet.
Split box	Lets you display two window panes of the same worksheet so that you can view two different areas at the same time.
Standard toolbar	Represents various shortcuts to menu commands, such as Open File, Save, Print, Cut, and so on, in button form.
Status bar	Contains information about options you have on or off, such as NUM (Num Lock) and CAPS (Caps Lock).
Title bar	Displays the name of the software and the name of the active workbook; either a default name such as Book1 or a saved file.
Workbook	An Excel file that contains one or more worksheets.
Worksheet frame	The row and column headings that appear along the top and left edge of the worksheet window.
Worksheet window	Contains the current worksheet—the work area.

Lesson 3: Getting Help

By now you have probably realized that you may run into problems as you work with your computer and Excel. If you find that you need a quick solution to a problem, you can use Excel's Help feature. The Help program is useful when you can't remember how to complete a task or when you just want to learn more about the software. Help makes it easy to find information on any topic that interests you.

In this lesson, you use the Excel Help program to learn more about how to get help while you are using Excel. Try using Excel's Help program now.

Lesson 3: Getting Help

To Get Help

1 **Click Help on the menu bar.**

The **H**elp menu displays a number of options that you can use to get help information.

2 **Choose the Microsoft Excel Help Topics command.**

The Excel Help Topics dialog box appears (see Figure 1.5). Here you can choose which of the four available Help functions you want to use: Contents, which displays a list of general topics; Index, which displays a comprehensive, alphabetical list of all topics; Find, which lets you search through all topics for a word or phrase; and Answer Wizard, which prompts you step-by-step through specific tasks.

Figure 1.5
Excel offers many ways to access useful help information.

3 **Click the Contents tab if it isn't already selected.**

This action ensures that the list of general Help topics is displayed (refer to Figure 1.5). The help information in the Contents tab is similar to a book with chapters—you display the chapter and read the pages.

4 **In the list of topics, click Getting Help, then click the Open button.**

This opens the topic, Getting Help. Specific tasks related to getting help appear in the topic list, as shown in Figure 1.6.

continues

Project 1 Getting Started with Excel

To Get Help (continued)

Figure 1.6
You can click any topic for more information.

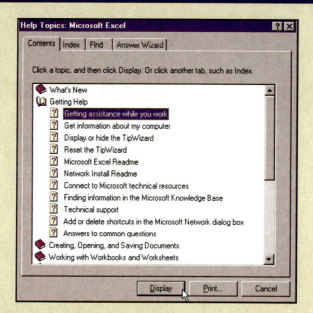

❺ **Click the topic Getting assistance while you work, and then click the Display button.**

A Help screen appears, providing access to information about how to get assistance while you work in Excel (see Figure 1.7).

Figure 1.7
In some Help screens, you can click labels for additional information.

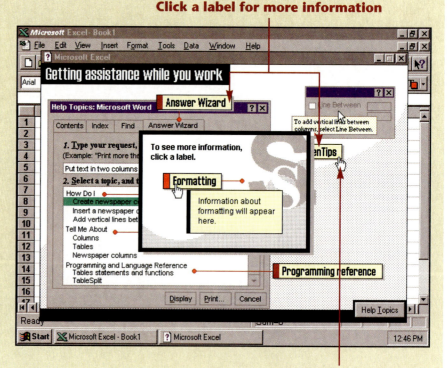

Lesson 3: Getting Help

6 Click the ScreenTips label.

A Help box appears, providing information about how to use the Excel ScreenTips feature while you work, as shown in Figure 1.8. Notice that when you move the mouse pointer to a label, the pointer becomes a hand with a pointing finger. This mouse pointer indicates that more information is available. Click any label on the Help screen to get information about using that feature.

Figure 1.8
Excel displays the specific information you require.

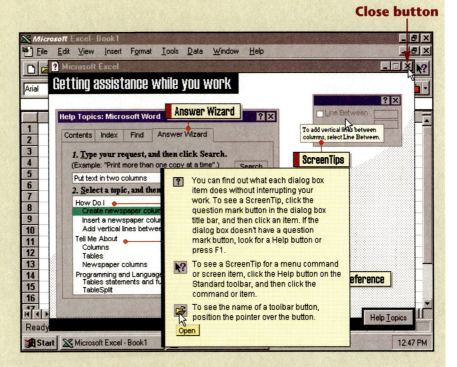

7 Click the Close button at the right end of the Help Topics title bar.

This closes Help and returns you to the worksheet. You are now ready to continue learning about how to use an Excel worksheet.

You can get help in Excel in many different ways. For quick help, you can press F1 at any time to display a Help window, or you can click the Help button on the Standard toolbar.

The AnswerWizard is an easy way to get step-by-step instructions for a specific task, such as how to turn on ToolTips. Choose Answer Wizard from the **H**elp menu, then follow the prompts that appear on your screen.

If you have used a previous version of Excel, choose **H**elp from the menu bar and explore What's New.

Remember, you can always print out the information in Help. The command to print can be found under the Options tab.

Lesson 4: Moving around the Worksheet

To use Excel, you need to learn how to move from one part of a worksheet to another. You can move around a worksheet using either the keyboard or the mouse. You probably will use a combination of these two methods.

Format
To change the appearance of text or numbers.

When you move around the worksheet, you usually go to a specific cell. When you get to that cell, it becomes the active cell so you can enter or edit information, *format* information, or otherwise change the contents of the cell.

Now use the default workbook on your screen to practice moving around Excel.

To Move around a Worksheet

1 **Move the mouse pointer to cell A9, and then click the left mouse button once.**

The border of cell A9 is highlighted in bold to indicate that it is the active cell (see Figure 1.9).

Figure 1.9
The active cell's address appears in the Name box in the Formula bar.

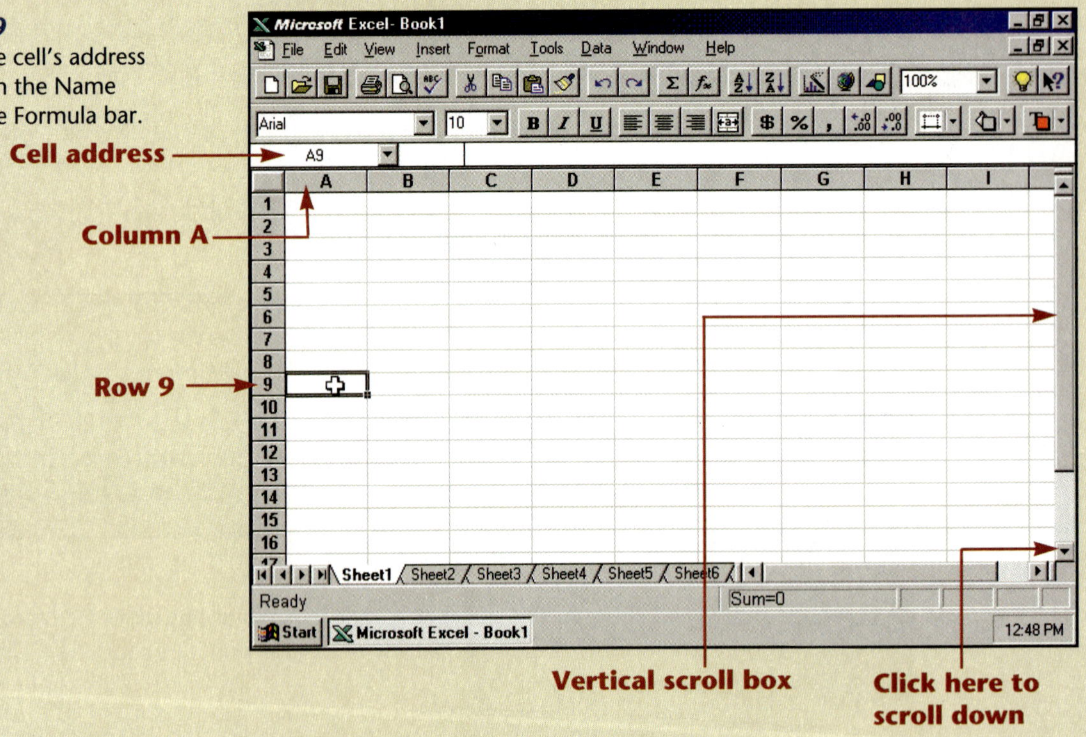

Cell address
Column A
Row 9
Vertical scroll box
Click here to scroll down

2 **Press ↑ three times.**

This moves the highlighting three rows up, making A6 the active cell.

3 **Press → three times.**

This moves the highlighting three columns to the right, making D6 the active cell.

Lesson 4: Moving around the Worksheet

④ Use the mouse to click in the vertical scroll bar, below the scroll box (refer to Figure 1.9).

Your view of the worksheet changes. Row 19 is now either at the top or near the top of the worksheet area, depending on your computer.

⑤ Click cell A19.

Cell A19 becomes the active cell. No matter which view of the worksheet is displayed on-screen, if you begin typing before you click a new cell, the text you enter will appear in the last active cell—in this case, cell D6.

⑥ Press Ctrl+G.

The Go To dialog box appears, as shown in Figure 1.10. In the Go To dialog box, you can specify the exact cell you want to make active. The key combination Ctrl+G means that you press and hold down Ctrl while you press G. This convention will be used to show key combinations throughout the rest of this book.

Figure 1.10
Use the Go To dialog box to make a specific cell active.

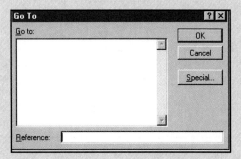

⑦ In the Reference text box, type r12, and then press ↵Enter.

The active cell is now R12.

⑧ Press Ctrl+G again.

The Go To dialog box appears. When you open the Go To dialog box again, the address of the last active cell appears in the **G**o to list box, with dollar signs ($) added before the row number and column letter. To go back to a cell you had been working in earlier, simply click it in the **G**o to list, then choose OK.

⑨ In the Reference text box, type aa6, and choose OK.

Cell AA6 becomes the active cell. You can also choose OK in the Go To dialog box to make the specified cell active.

⑩ Press Ctrl+Home.

Your view of the worksheet changes and A1—the first cell in the worksheet—becomes the active cell again.

continues

Project 1 Getting Started with Excel

> **To Move around a Worksheet** (continued)
>
> Keep this worksheet open for the next lesson, in which you begin entering data. Table 1.2 lists other keystrokes for moving around a worksheet.

Table 1.2 Moving around a Worksheet Using the Keyboard

Press	To Move
↑, ↓, ←, or →	One cell in direction of arrow (up, down, left, or right).
PgUp or PgDn	One screen up or down.
Home	To the first cell of the current row.
Ctrl+Home	To the first cell of the active worksheet—A1.
Ctrl+→	To the last or first cell in a range of contiguous cells—to the right—stops at Column IV—(256 columns).
Ctrl+←	To the first cell in a range of contiguous cells—to the left—stops at Column A.
Ctrl+↑	To the first cell in a range of contiguous cells—to the top—stops at Row 1.
Ctrl+↓	To the last cell in a range of contiguous cells—to the bottom—stops at row 16,384—(the bottom row).
Ctrl+PgUp	To the preceding worksheet. You can also click the Sheet tab.
Ctrl+PgDn	To the following worksheet. You can also click the Sheet tab.

Lesson 5: Entering Data

Now that you have had a chance to find your way around the Excel screen, it's time to create your own worksheet. *Values*, *text*, and *formulas* are referred to as data and can be entered in the cells of your worksheet. In this lesson, you set up a simple worksheet to track office expenses. You also use a formula, one of the most powerful features of Excel, to find the total amount of the expenses.

Try creating the expense worksheet now.

Jargon Watch

If you are not used to working with numbers, you may not be familiar with some of the terms used to describe spreadsheets. Values and formulas are terms borrowed from math that apply to even the simplest work you will do with a spreadsheet.

The formal terms are used here simply to let you know what they are and what they mean. A **value** is a number you enter in a cell of a worksheet. **Text** is any word or label you enter in the spreadsheet. A **formula** is a specific calculation that Excel performs, such as adding or subtracting two numbers.

Lesson 5: Entering Data

To Enter Data

1 **In the default workbook (Book1) that you used in the previous lesson, click cell A2.**

A2 becomes the active cell. Information you type will appear in this cell. You can now enter the first item on your office expense worksheet.

2 **Type Rent.**

As you type in the cell, a blinking vertical cursor appears. Characters that you type appear to the left of the cursor. Also, as you type in the worksheet cell, the word also appears in the Formula bar (see Figure 1.11). You can type directly in the Formula bar by clicking in the cell, then clicking in the Formula bar.

Notice that when the mouse pointer is positioned within the formula bar, or within the cell while you are typing, it changes to an *I-beam*. You can use the I-beam to position the cursor for entering or editing data.

Notice that three buttons appear on the Formula bar. The red X is the Cancel button. Clicking the Cancel button is the same as pressing Esc when you are typing data into a cell; that is, Excel stops accepting the entry and the cell's previous contents reappear. The green check mark is the Enter button. Clicking the Enter button accepts the data you entered as complete. You learn about the Formula Wizard button in Project 4.

I-beam
The mouse pointer changes to an I-beam when placed in an area in which you can enter text or other data, including worksheet cells and the Formula bar.

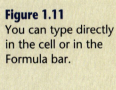

Figure 1.11
You can type directly in the cell or in the Formula bar.

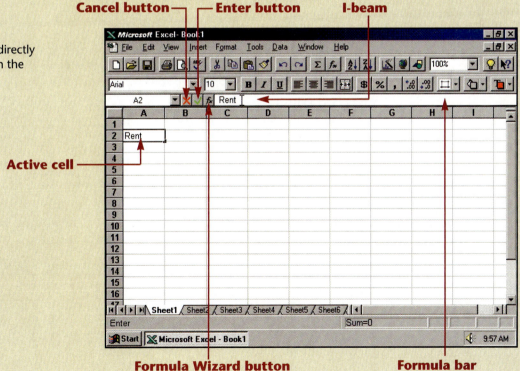

continues

Project 1 Getting Started with Excel

To Enter Data (continued)

> **If you have problems...**
>
> If you make a mistake while typing, press [Backspace] to delete the error, and then continue typing. If you move on to another cell and then discover a mistake, click the mouse or use the arrow keys to highlight the cell with the mistake, double-click to select the cell, and then use the arrow keys, [Backspace], or [Del] to correct the mistake. If you want to replace the entire contents of the cell, double-click the cell so that it is in edit mode, and then begin typing; the new text you enter replaces the cell's previous contents.

❸ Press [↓].

The text you typed is entered in cell A2, and A3 becomes the active cell. You can now enter the other expenses in your worksheet. You can also press [Enter] to enter information and move to the next cell down the column, or you can click the Enter button on the Formula bar to enter the information and remain in the same cell.

❹ Enter the following additional expenses in your worksheet. Press [↓] or [Enter] after typing each word to enter the data and move to the next cell down the column.

> **Supplies**
> **Phone**
> **Cleaning**
> **Miscellaneous**
> **Total**

Each time you press [↓] or [Enter], the text is entered in the active cell and the cell below becomes the active cell. You have now entered all the various expenses you will track in this office expense worksheet. The word Total should appear in cell A7 and cell A8 should be active. Now you can enter the amount paid for the rent last month.

❺ Click in cell B2, type 1200, and then press [↓].

Be sure to press [↓] or [Enter] to enter the information. Now enter the amounts for the rest of your expenses. (Don't worry that your numeric entries don't show dollar signs right now; in Project 3, you learn how to format numbers to show dollar signs.)

❻ Type each of the following amounts and press [↓] or [Enter] to enter them into the worksheet:

> 300
> 150
> 80
> 75

Lesson 5: Entering Data

You have now entered a record of your expenses into the worksheet. To see how useful a spreadsheet can be, try entering a simple formula to find the monthly total for the expenses in this example.

❼ Click in cell B7 and type =b2+b3+b4+b5+b6.

You have now typed the formula for adding all the expenses in column B. The equals sign identifies the information as a formula instead of data to be entered in the cell. This formula tells Excel to add the contents of the five cells in column B. Because the formula is entered in cell B7, that is where the total will be displayed.

❽ Click the Enter button (the green check mark) on the Formula bar to enter the formula.

You can also press ↵Enter or ↓ to enter the formula. Excel adds the numbers and displays the result in cell B7 with the total for the expenses. Notice that as long as cell B7 is active, the formula—not the actual numerical total—appears in the Formula bar (see Figure 1.12). If necessary, click cell B7 to make it active so you can see the contents of the Formula bar.

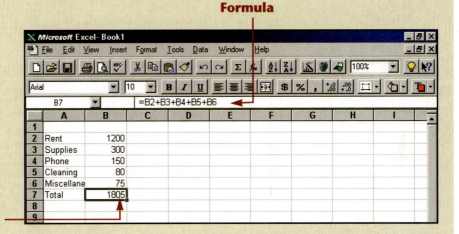

Figure 1.12
The expense total appears in cell B7 while the formula appears in the Formula bar

Result of formula

The true power of Excel resides in formulas. If several of your expenses change next month, you can find the new expense total simply by entering the new information in the correct cells. The formula in B7 automatically calculates a new total for you.

Try changing one of the expense values now.

❾ Click cell B4.

This makes cell B4 the active cell.

❿ Type 100, and then press ↵Enter.

Notice that when you enter the new amount in cell B4, the total automatically changes in cell B7.

Keep this office expense worksheet open for the next lesson, where you learn how to save your work.

Project 1 Getting Started with Excel

Lesson 6: Saving a Worksheet

Up to this point, none of the information that you have entered in your expense worksheet has been safely stored for future use. At the moment, your worksheet and the workbook that contains it are stored in the computer's *random access memory*, or *RAM*. If your computer were to crash—or shut down—for any reason, you would lose your expense worksheet.

For this reason, it is important to save your work every 10 to 15 minutes. You can save your work to the *hard disk* inside the computer or to a *floppy disk* that you insert and can take with you. You may already be familiar with the concepts and terms described above. If not, see the Jargon Watch later in this lesson.

File
Information you enter in your computer and save for future use, such as a document or workbook.

When you save a workbook, or *file*, you assign the file a name and location on disk. Later, you can retrieve the file and add to it, edit it, and print it. So that you don't lose any of your valuable work (and your valuable time), save your expense worksheet now.

To Save a Worksheet

❶ Choose File from the menu bar.

The **File** pull-down menu opens.

❷ Choose the Save command.

The Save As dialog box opens, as shown in Figure 1.13. The first time you save a file, choosing either **Save** or Save **As** opens the Save As dialog box. Notice that the text in the File **n**ame text box is highlighted; this is the temporary file name that Excel assigns to your workbook.

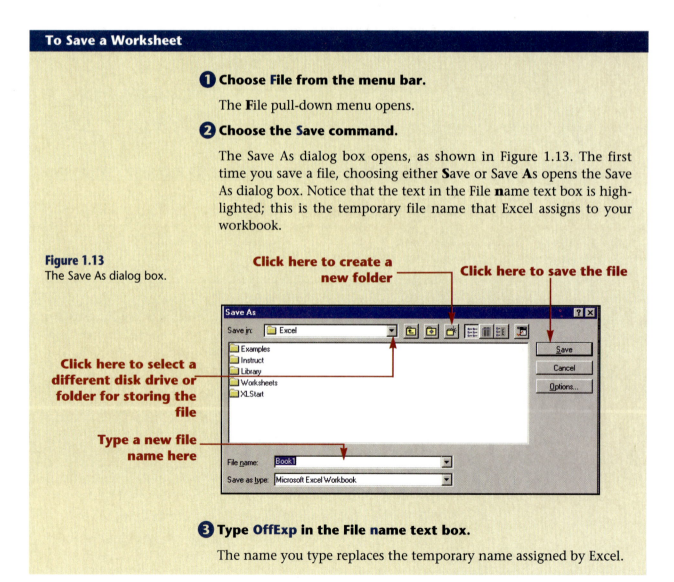

Figure 1.13
The Save As dialog box.

❸ Type OffExp in the File name text box.

The name you type replaces the temporary name assigned by Excel.

Lesson 6: Saving a Worksheet

You can type any name you want using Windows 95's file-naming rules. You can include spaces as well as upper- and lowercase letters. Excel automatically stores the file in the default Excel file format, adding the XLS file extension, but by default, Windows 95 does not show file extensions.

❹ Click the Save in drop-down arrow, then click the drive or folder where you want to save your workbook.

In the Save As dialog box, Excel automatically proposes to save the workbook in the current drive (usually C) and in the default folder, Excel. Ask your instructor where to save the files you create during this course. If you want to save to a different drive, such as a floppy disk, select the drive from the Save in list. If you want to save the file in a different folder, select the folder from the Save in list, or click the New Folder button to create and name a new folder.

> **If you have problems...**
>
> If you try to save to a floppy disk and you get an error message, check two things: First, be sure to select the correct disk drive—most likely drive A. Second, be sure that you are using a formatted disk. If you aren't using a formatted disk, you should see an error message that tells you the disk you selected is not formatted. The error message may ask if you want to format the disk now. If this is the case, and you want to format the disk so you can save files to it, click the **Y**es button and follow the instructions until the disk formatting is complete.
>
> Be careful when formatting disks, and make sure that you don't format your hard disk drive. When you format a disk, all information stored on the disk is erased. If you have any questions about formatting or disk drives, don't hesitate to ask your instructor for help.

❺ Choose Save.

This saves a copy of your workbook containing the worksheet data as a file named OffExp. The Save As dialog box closes and the new file name appears in the workbook window title bar. Now practice a shortcut method for quickly saving a file that already has a name, drive, and folder.

❻ Click the Save button on the toolbar.

This method quickly saves your workbook. Alternatively, you can press Ctrl+S. If you want to save an existing workbook with a different name or to a different drive or folder, choose Save **A**s from the **F**ile menu.

Keep the OffExp workbook open for the next lesson, where you learn how to print your work.

Jargon Watch

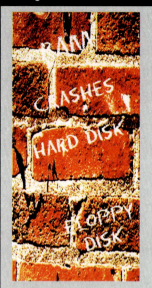

In this lesson, a number of technical terms have been used to describe how computers save information. **RAM** stands for **random access memory**, which simply means the temporary storage space that the computer uses for programs and data it's currently working with.

When a computer **crashes**, it means that an error—either in a program the computer is running or in the hardware or power supply—has caused the computer to stop working. Everything stored in RAM is lost when a crash occurs. Remember, it's important to frequently save your work to a **hard disk** or a **floppy disk**.

Floppy disks are small disks that you can carry around with you. They can be either 5 1/4-inch disks or 3 1/2-inch disks, and are often used to keep backup copies of important information. Although 3 1/2-inch floppy disks have hard outer cases, the disk inside is flexible. Your hard disk is built into your PC, and is made up of several rigid platters that look similar to the CDs that you buy in music stores. The bulk of the programs and information that your computer uses is stored on the computer's hard disk.

Lesson 7: Printing a Worksheet

Current worksheet
The worksheet containing the active cell.

Now that you have saved your workbook and worksheet, you can print a copy of your worksheet for your files or to review away from the computer. It's a good idea to save documents immediately before printing them, as you did in Lesson 6. Now print your expense worksheet—the *current worksheet*.

To Print a Worksheet

1 Make sure that the printer is turned on, has paper, and is on-line.

On-line
Directly connected to a computer and ready for use.

You can't print if the printer is not turned on, if the printer is out of paper, or if the printer is not on-line. Printers often have a light that shows whether the printer is on-line, or receiving commands from the computer. If the printer is not on-line, Excel displays an error message.

2 From the File menu, choose Print.

The Print dialog box appears, as shown in Figure 1.14.

Figure 1.14
You can change any of the options in the Print dialog box.

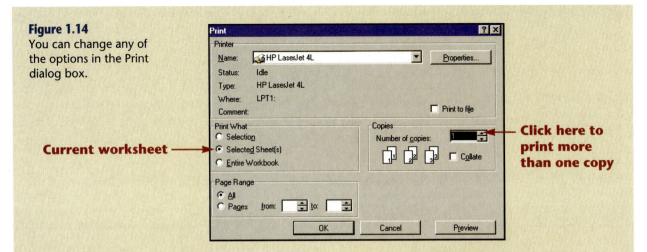

❸ In the Copies text box, click the up triangle once.

This changes the number of copies to be printed to **2**. You can also change other options in the Print dialog box. After the printer is ready, you should check the worksheet you are going to print.

❹ Click the Preview button in the Print dialog box.

The worksheet now appears in the Print Preview window, which lets you see how the entire worksheet will look when printed (see Figure 1.15). When the mouse pointer changes to a magnifying glass, you can click within the window to increase the size of the document being displayed.

Figure 1.15
View the worksheet as it will look when printed to decide if you need to make changes.

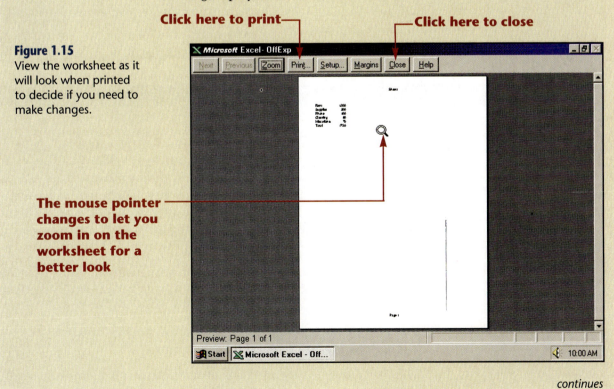

continues

To Print a Worksheet (continued)

5 **Click anywhere in the worksheet.**

Your view of the worksheet becomes enlarged so that you can more easily read it, but you can't see the entire page. You can click the worksheet again to go back to the view of the whole page. If you decide you want to make a change in the worksheet before you print it, click the **C**lose button to close the view and return to the worksheet in Excel.

6 **Click the Print button on the Print Preview toolbar.**

Excel sends two copies of your worksheet to the printer.

To quickly open the Print dialog box, press Ctrl+P.

To quickly print the current worksheet without opening the Print dialog box, click the Print button on the Standard toolbar.

To change to Print Preview without opening the Print dialog box, click the Print Preview button on the Standard toolbar, or choose Print Pre**v**iew from the **F**ile menu.

Lesson 8: Exiting Excel

Before you turn off your computer, you should first close the file you have created and then exit Excel so that you don't lose any of your work. Complete this project by closing your file and exiting the Excel and Windows software.

To Exit Excel

1 **From the File menu, choose Exit.**

If you haven't saved your work, Excel displays a dialog box that asks if you would like to save your work. Choosing **Y**es saves all active files that have been named, and then closes the program. Choosing **N**o closes the program and deletes any work left on-screen. After you save your work and close Excel, the Windows Desktop appears if no other software applications are running.

If you have completed your session on the computer, proceed with step 2. Otherwise, continue with the "Applying Your Skills" section at the end of this project.

2 **To exit Windows, click the Start button on the taskbar and choose Shut Down from the Start menu.**

The Shut Down Windows dialog box appears, asking you to confirm that you are ready to shut down Windows and your computer.

③ Verify that the Shut Down the Computer? option button is selected, then choose Yes.

Windows closes and prepares your computer for shut down. When a message appears telling you that it is safe to shut off your computer, you may do so.

To exit any file or program you are currently using, you can also click the Close button at the right end of the window's title. For example, clicking the Close button of a workbook closes the workbook, and clicking the Close button in the Excel title bar closes Excel. Again, you are prompted to save unsaved work before you close any file or software.

Project Summary

To	Do This
Start Excel	Click the Start button on the Windows taskbar, move the mouse pointer to **P**rograms on the Start menu, then choose Microsoft Excel from the Programs nested menu.
Make a cell active	Click it.
Get Help	Open the **H**elp menu and choose **H**elp Topics for general information, or Answer Wizard to ask a specific question.
Move to cell A1	Press Ctrl+Home.
Enter data in a cell	Click the cell, type the data, then press ↵Enter.
Enter a formula in a cell	Click the cell, type an equals sign, type the formula, then press ↵Enter.
Save a worksheet	Choose **F**ile, **S**ave. If necessary, type the file name in the File **n**ame text box, select a disk drive and folder from the Save **i**n list, then choose **S**ave.
Print a worksheet	Click the Print button on the Standard toolbar.
Preview a worksheet before printing	Click the Print Preview button on the standard toolbar.

Applying Your Skills

At the end of each project in Excel for Windows 95 Essentials, you can learn how to apply your Excel skills to various business situations. The following exercises enable you to practice the skills you have learned in this project. Take a few minutes to work through these exercises now.

Creating an Employee List

Imagine that you are the owner and hands-on business manager of Sound Byte Music, a new store located in a college town. With Excel, you can keep track of the employees you hire and plan to hire. You can list job descriptions, hire date, starting salary, and raise information.

To Create an Employee List

1. Start Windows and then start Microsoft Excel.
2. Use the default worksheet.
3. Enter the following row labels, starting in cell A3 and moving down to cell A6:

    Office Manager

    Sales Clerk

    Stock Clerk

    Cashier

    You can add your own categories to the list if you want.

4. After you have finished setting up the row labels, enter the following column labels, starting in cell A2 and moving to the right to cell F2:

    Position

    Description

    Salary

    Employee name

    Start Date

    Next Review Date

5. If you want, enter a formula in cell C7 to calculate your total projected salary costs.
6. Save the file as **Job List**. If requested by your instructor, print two copies of the file. Then close it.

Creating an Advertising Worksheet

One of your first goals in launching Sound Byte Music is to let people know about the store and that it is open for business. Create a worksheet to help you manage the costs and benefits of the advertising campaign by listing the various types of advertising, when the ad was run, its cost, and its effect on business.

To Create the Advertising Worksheet

1. Start Windows and then start Microsoft Excel.
2. Use the default worksheet.

Applying Your Skills

3. Enter the following column labels, starting in cell A2, moving from left to right:

   Title

   Medium

   Date

   Cost

   Effect

   You can also add your own categories to this list.

4. After you have finished setting up the column labels, enter the following example information, starting in cell A3, moving from left to right:

   Welcome

   Radio

   9/27/95

   $400

   $750

5. Create your own information for a newspaper ad and a television ad in rows 4 and 5.

6. Use formulas to total the amounts in the Cost column and in the Effect column.

7. Save the file as **Ad Budget**. If requested by your instructor, print two copies of the file. Then close it.

Starting an Office Budget

You can also use Excel to keep a handle on office expenses. Create a spreadsheet to help you plan office expenses by listing the costs of typical stationery items you require to get started.

To Create the Office Budget

1. Start Windows and then start Microsoft Excel.

2. Use the default worksheet.

3. Enter the following row labels, starting in cell A2 and moving down to cell A6:

   Letterhead

   Business Cards

   Envelopes

   Mailing Labels

   Total

   You can add your own categories to the list if you want.

4. After you have finished setting up the row labels, enter the following costs, starting in cell B2 and moving down to cell B5:

    250

    175

    125

    150

5. Enter a formula in cell B7 to calculate the total costs.

6. Save the file as **Paper Costs**. If requested by your instructor, print two copies of the file. Then close it.

Cataloging Your Music

You can use an Excel worksheet to create a catalog of your CD and cassette tape collection. (You may even have some old records that you want to include.) List each CD or cassette by artist in the left column of your worksheet, then add columns for title, label, type of music, and price. You can also list the release year, favorite song titles, and the length of the entire CD or tape in separate columns.

In Project 6, you learn how to sort items in a list. You will then be able to sort this catalog by any of the types of information you include.

To Create the Music Catalog

1. Start Windows and then start Microsoft Excel.

2. Use the default worksheet.

3. Enter the labels and information to create a list of your music CDs and cassette tapes. Use as many of the suggested categories as you want and feel free to add your own.

4. Enter a formula to find the total amount you have spent on your music collection.

5. Save the file as **Music Collection**. If requested by your instructor, print two copies. Then close it.

Scheduling Classes

An Excel spreadsheet can also help you keep track of your classes and class times. Create a worksheet that lists the courses you would like to take this year, along with the semester the course is offered, the time the course is offered, the professor, and whether the course counts toward your major. In later projects, you can add your grades to the worksheet and calculate your grade point average.

To Create the Schedule

1. Start Windows and then start Microsoft Excel.
2. Use the default worksheet.
3. Enter the labels and information to create a list of classes. Use as many of the suggested categories as you want and feel free to add your own.
4. Save the file as **Course List**. If requested by your instructor, print two copies. Then close it.

Checking Your Skills

True/False

For each of the following, check *T* or *F* to indicate whether the statement is true or false.

__T __F **1.** The Formula bar of the Excel screen displays the contents of the current cell and the cell's address.

__T __F **2.** Pressing F1 displays the Excel Help screen.

__T __F **3.** The only way to move around a worksheet is by using the mouse.

__T __F **4.** You can create a new folder for storing a file in the Save As dialog box.

__T __F **5.** You can press Ctrl+S or click the Save button on the toolbar to save changes to a file that has already been named.

Multiple Choice

Circle the letter of the correct answer for each of the following.

1. Which of the following is *not* a part of the Microsoft Excel screen?
    a. ruler line
    b. sheet tab
    c. status bar
    d. toolbar

2. Which of the following is a valid cell address?
    a. b-12
    b. B:12
    c. B12
    d. B/12

3. If your active cell is F6, which of the following keys does *not* move you to a new position in a worksheet?

   a. Home

   b. End

   c. PgUp

   d. Tab

4. Which of the following is an example of a formula?

   a. $240

   b. =B2+B3+B4

   c. January

   d. 1/21/94

5. Which of the following is *not* a method of getting Help in Excel?

   a. AnswerWizard

   b. Help button

   c. Tell Me More

   d. ScreenTips

Completion

In the blank provided, write the correct answer for each of the following statements.

1. To enter text or numbers in a cell you can press _____ or a directional arrow key.

2. To use a button on the toolbar, you _____ the button.

3. The Name box in the Formula bar displays the_____.

4. To select a range of cells, you can use the mouse to click and drag or you can use the _____ and arrow keys.

5. To boldface text, use the _____ toolbar.

Checking Your Skills

Screen ID
Label each element of the Excel screen in Figure 1.16.

1. _____
2. _____
3. _____
4. _____
5. _____
6. _____
7. _____
8. _____
9. _____
10. _____
11. _____

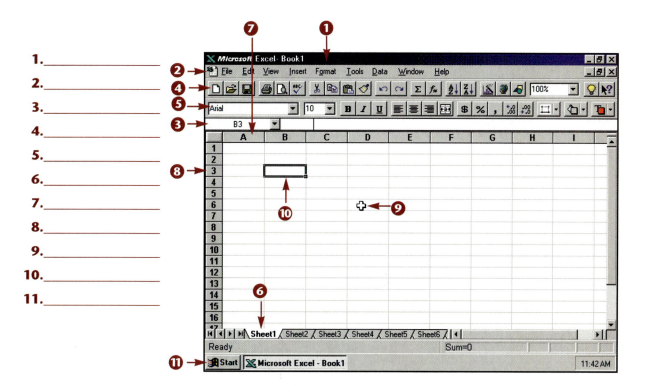

Project 2

Building A Spreadsheet

Creating an Office Expense Budget

In this project, you learn how to
- Open an Existing Worksheet
- Select Worksheet Items
- Use Autofill
- Add and Remove Rows and Columns
- Copy Information
- Move Information
- Create Formulas
- Copy Formulas

Project 2   Building A Spreadsheet

Why Would I Do This?

Now that you are familiar with the Excel screen and the basics of entering data and saving files, it's time to work with Excel's most powerful tools. In Project 1, you learned how to create a simple worksheet. In this project, you learn to use Excel to create a Budget worksheet that includes office expense information for several months and calculates monthly totals.

The sample information in the Budget worksheet will show you how formulas in an Excel worksheet can be used to manage your office finances. You also learn how to use the editing features of Excel as you create your worksheet. To complete the lessons in this project, Excel for Windows 95 should be up and running on your computer.

Lesson 1: Opening an Existing Worksheet

Once you create a workbook and save it to your hard disk or floppy disk, you can open the workbook again to resume working with the worksheet data that it contains. With Excel, you can open a new workbook file, open an existing workbook file, or work with the default workbook. The default worksheet appears on-screen whenever you start Excel, or when you create a new file using the General Workbook file template.

In this lesson, you open an existing workbook file that contains the worksheet data you will use throughout this project.

To Open an Existing Worksheet

1 Start Excel if it is not already running, and in the default workbook file, click the File menu.

The File menu opens to display a number of commands.

2 Choose the Open command.

The Open dialog box appears, as shown in Figure 2.1. The files and folders stored in the default folder—Excel—are displayed. You can also click the Open File button on the Standard toolbar to get to the Open dialog box.

Lesson 1: Opening an Existing Worksheet

Figure 2.1
The Open dialog box lists all files in the default folder.

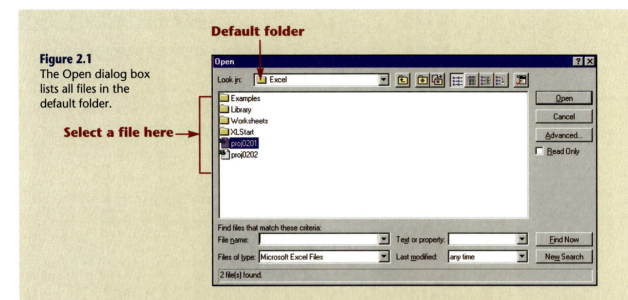

❸ **In the list of files and folders, click the Proj0201 file icon to select it.**

This file may already be selected. If you don't see Proj0201 in the list, try opening another folder from the Look in drop-down list, or looking on another drive. The file may be stored in a different location on your system. If you can't find the file on your computer, ask your instructor for the location of the data files you will use with this book.

> **If you have problems...**
>
> If, when you click the file to select it, the characters in the file name become highlighted instead of the entire file name, it means you changed to Rename mode. In Rename mode, you can change the name of an existing file or folder. To select the file, make sure you click the file icon.

❹ **Choose Open.**

The office budget sample worksheet (Proj0201) appears on-screen, as shown in Figure 2.2. Now save this sample file under a more descriptive file name to keep the original data file intact.

continues

Project 2 Building A Spreadsheet

To Open an Existing Worksheet (continued)

Figure 2.2
Save the sample file Proj0201 as Budget to use in this project.

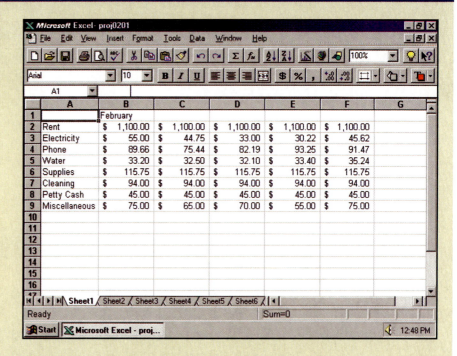

❺ Choose the File menu again, then choose the Save As command.

The Save As dialog box appears.

❻ In the File name text box, type Budget to replace Proj0201.

Budget is the workbook file name that will be used throughout the rest of this project.

❼ From the Save in drop-down list, select the appropriate drive and folder for saving the new file.

If necessary, ask your instructor where you should save the new workbook file.

❽ Choose Save.

Excel saves the workbook as Budget and automatically closes the original data file. Keep the Budget workbook open to use in the next lesson.

 To open a file quickly from the Open dialog box, double-click the file icon in the list of files. If you double-click the file name, however, you may end up in Rename mode.

Lesson 2: Selecting Worksheet Items

Selecting
Designating an item on-screen. You select an item so that you can do something with it. Also called *highlighting*.

In order to build a worksheet, you must learn how to *select* items in the worksheet. When you select an item, you highlight that item so that you can make changes to it. You select a cell, for example, so that you can copy the cell's contents into another cell. You must select a column so that you can change the column's width.

In this lesson, you learn how to select items in the Budget worksheet.

To Select Worksheet Items

❶ Click cell A1 in the Budget worksheet.

You have selected cell A1 by clicking in it. Once you select a cell, the cell border is highlighted in bold, the cell's address appears in the name box of the Formula bar, and the cell's contents appear in the contents area of the Formula bar.

❷ Click cell A2, press and hold down the left mouse button, then drag the mouse pointer to cell G2. Release the left mouse button when the mouse pointer is in cell G2.

Range
A cell or a rectangular group of adjacent cells.

Several cells are now selected. As you drag the mouse, the name box on the Formula bar shows you how many rows and columns you are selecting. When you finish selecting the cells, the cells are highlighted and the first cell address appears in the name box (see Figure 2.3). Dragging the mouse is an easy way to select a range of cells.

Now practice selecting an entire column of the worksheet.

Figure 2.3
The first selected cell appears active while the rest of the selected cells are highlighted.

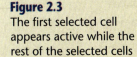

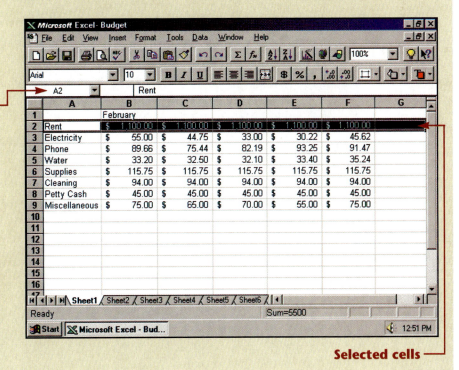

continues

Project 2 Building A Spreadsheet

To Select Worksheet Items   (continued)

Worksheet frame
The horizontal bar containing the column letters and the vertical bar containing the row numbers, located in the worksheet area.

❸ **Click the column heading B in the *worksheet frame*.**

This selects the entire worksheet column B, as shown in Figure 2.4. Keep the Budget worksheet open to use in the next lesson.

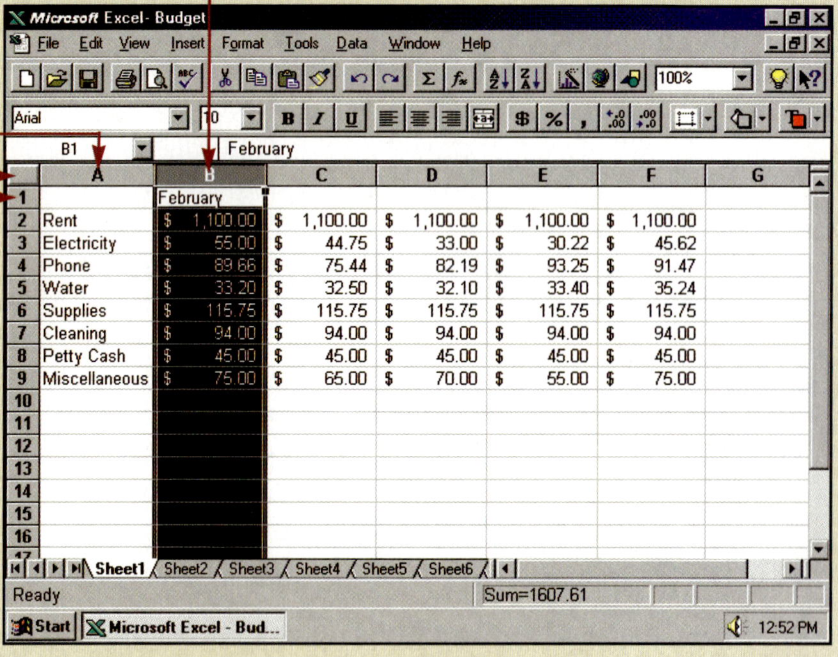

Figure 2.4
You can quickly select a column or row by clicking the column or row heading in the worksheet frame.

Click the Select All button to select the entire worksheet

You can select two or more rows, columns, or cells by pressing and holding down Ctrl while you click the individual elements. This way, you don't have to select rows, columns, or cells in succession.

To select the entire worksheet, click the Select All button (the gray rectangle) in the top left corner of the worksheet frame.

You can also double-click a cell to display the I-beam; then drag the I-beam across any part of the text or data in the cell to select it. This method is handy for working with part of the contents of a cell.

With the keyboard, you can quickly select text using the ⇧Shift key and the arrow keys. Position the insertion point where you want to start selecting, press and hold down ⇧Shift, then use the arrow keys to move the insertion point to the last item you want to select.

Lesson 3: Using AutoFill

You have now opened the Budget worksheet and practiced selecting items in the worksheet. The Budget worksheet has information on various expenses over several months, but before the worksheet is complete, a number of items need to be changed.

As you can see, row 1 of the Budget worksheet should have column headings for each month of expenses you track. Using the AutoFill command, you can easily select a range of cells to have Excel fill the range with a sequence of information.

In this case, by selecting the cell containing the label February and then selecting a range of cells, you can extend a sequence of months (such as February, March, April) to the range you select. You can also set up a sequence of numbers, letters, and days of the week using the AutoFill command.

To Use the AutoFill Command

❶ Click cell B1 in the Budget worksheet.

Cell B1 contains the column heading for the month of February. To build column headings for the rest of the worksheet, you select this cell as the starting value for the fill. This also tells Excel the type of series you want to create—in this case, a series of consecutive months.

❷ Move the mouse pointer to the lower right corner of cell B1 until the pointer changes to a black cross.

When the mouse pointer changes to a black cross, also called the *fill handle*, Excel confirms that it is ready to select a range of cells to be filled (see Figure 2.5).

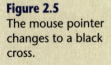

Figure 2.5
The mouse pointer changes to a black cross.

continues

To Use the AutoFill Command (continued)

❸ Press the left mouse button and drag right to cell F1, then release the mouse button.

This action selects the range B1 through F1. When you release the mouse button, Excel fills the range with months (starting from February and increasing by one month for each cell in the range), as shown in Figure 2.6.

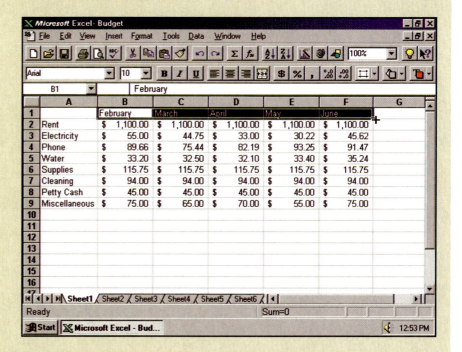

Figure 2.6
Using the AutoFill command to create a series of months.

❹ Click any cell.

This deselects the range. From here you can take the next step to build your Budget worksheet: adding and deleting columns and rows. Save your changes and keep the worksheet open for the next lesson.

If you have problems...

If you select cells already containing data to AutoFill, Excel overwrites the data in the cells. You can reverse this action by choosing **E**dit, **U**ndo before performing any other action.

Lesson 4: Adding and Removing Rows and Columns

If you want to create a sequence of consecutive increments to fill by example (1, 2, 3, and so on), you enter the first item in the sequence and select that cell. If you want to create a sequence of values other than 1 (5, 10, 15), you enter the data in two cells and select those cells before filling the range.

You may already have noticed that sometimes Excel seems to anticipate what you are going to enter into a cell. For example, you may start typing a column label, and Excel automatically completes the word you have begun—sometimes correctly, and sometimes incorrectly. This is a feature called AutoComplete. With AutoComplete, as you enter new data Excel considers data you have recently entered to see if they seem to match. If so, Excel automatically enters the same data you entered previously. For example, if you enter the label *Winter* in a cell, then start typing *Wi* into another cell, Excel will automatically assume you are entering *Winter* again. If you are, this saves you some typing. If you aren't, you can edit the entry.

To disable AutoComplete, choose **O**ptions from the **T**ools menu, click the Edit tab, and deselect the Enable Auto**C**omplete for Cell Values check box. Then choose OK.

Lesson 4: Adding and Removing Rows and Columns

If you decide to add more information to your worksheet, Excel allows you to add rows and columns. You may, for example, want to add expense information for the month of January to your worksheet. Also, the cost of insurance, a common expense, is not listed in your worksheet. If you no longer want to include certain information, you can also remove columns and rows.

To Add and Remove Rows and Columns

Now use the Budget worksheet to practice adding and removing rows and columns.

❶ Click the row 8 row heading in the Budget worksheet frame.

The entire row 8 is highlighted to show that it has been selected.

❷ From the Insert menu, choose Rows.

The contents of row 8 and all rows below it move down one row. A new, blank row is inserted as row 8 (see Figure 2.7).

❸ Type Insurance in cell A8, and then press ↵Enter.

continues

To Add and Remove Rows and Columns (continued)

Figure 2.7
A new, blank row inserted into the Budget worksheet.

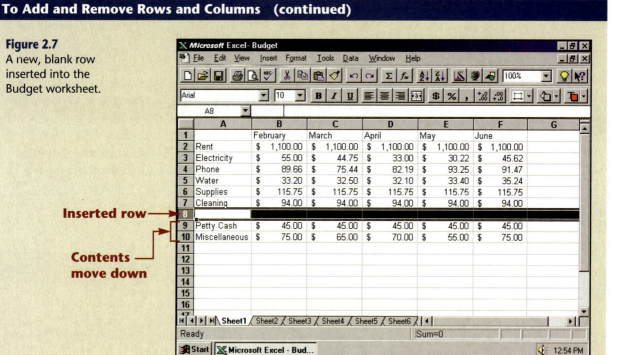

You have inserted and labeled a new row for insurance expenses. Now insert a new column for January's expenses.

④ Click the column B heading in the worksheet frame.

The entire column B is highlighted to show that it has been selected.

⑤ From the Insert menu, choose Columns.

The contents of column B, and all columns to the right of column B, move to the right and a blank column B is added to the worksheet.

⑥ Type January in cell B1, and then press ↵Enter.

You have inserted and labeled a new row for January expenses. Finally, you decide that you don't want to include what have been listed as Petty Cash expenses in your worksheet. Delete the entire row 9 to remove Petty Cash expenses from your worksheet.

⑦ Click the row 9 row heading in the worksheet frame.

The entire row 9, Petty Cash expenses, is highlighted.

⑧ From the Edit menu, choose Delete.

Row 9 is now deleted. When you delete a selected column or row, you also delete any contents in that column or row. Your worksheet should now look similar to Figure 2.8. Save your changes and leave the Budget worksheet open to use in the next lesson.

Lesson 4: Adding and Removing Rows and Columns

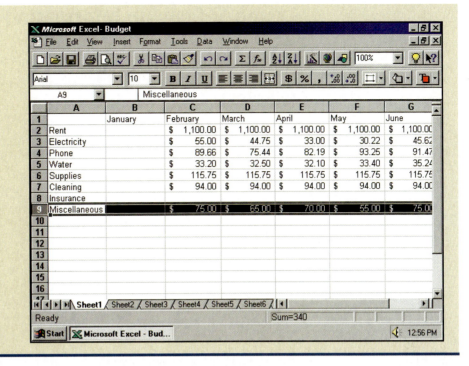

Figure 2.8
Use the **E**dit **D**elete command to remove unwanted columns or rows.

If you want to insert more than one row or column at a time, select as many adjacent rows or columns as you need blank rows or columns, and then choose **I**nsert, **R**ows or **C**olumns. For example, if you want to insert five new rows beginning at row 4, select rows 4 through 8, and then choose **I**nsert, **R**ows. The same is true for deleting rows and columns. To delete five columns, select the five columns you want to delete, and then choose **E**dit, **D**elete.

You can use shortcut menus to insert or delete columns and rows. Select the item you want to insert or delete, move the mouse pointer to it and click the right mouse button. Choose the appropriate command from the shortcut menu that appears.

If you change your mind about what you added or deleted, open the **E**dit menu and choose the **U**ndo command. Undo reverses the last action you performed.

If you have problems...

If the Delete dialog box appears when you choose **E**dit, **D**elete, it means that you didn't select the entire row or column before choosing the command. You can either cancel the dialog box and try selecting the row again, or select Entire **R**ow or Entire **C**olumn in the dialog box and choose OK to complete the deletion. The same is true for inserting and deleting rows and columns.

Lesson 5: Copying Information

By adding and removing columns and rows, you have made some important changes to your Budget worksheet. You still need to insert expense information, however, in the new row for Insurance and the new column for January.

Because you don't have the exact information for your office's insurance bills or for your January expenses in this example, assume that you can use information from other parts of your worksheet to estimate these parts of your Budget. You might assume, for example, that January expenses are the same as your February expenses. Instead of retyping the February information, you can copy the cells from the February column to the January column.

Copying information from one column to another is much quicker than typing it a second time. You can copy and move text, numbers, and formulas from one cell to another, from one worksheet to another, and from one file to another. Use the Budget worksheet to practice copying and moving data.

To Copy Information

❶ In the Budget worksheet, select cells C2 through C9.

This highlights the expense information that you want to copy from the February column into the January column.

❷ From the Edit menu, choose Copy.

A copy of the selected cell's contents is placed in the Windows *Clipboard*. The Clipboard stores information or formulas you want to move or copy to another location (see the Jargon Watch later in this project, to find out more about the Clipboard).

❸ Click cell B2.

This selects the location where you want the copied information to appear. You do not have to select a range that is the same size as the range you are copying; Excel automatically fills in the data starting with the one cell you select.

❹ From the Edit menu, choose Paste.

The copied cell's contents appear in cells B2 through B9, as shown in Figure 2.9. Note that the expense information in the January column is exactly the same as the information in the February column. To estimate your office's insurance expense, assume for now that your monthly insurance bill is the same as your monthly office rent payment.

Lesson 5: Copying Information

Figure 2.9
The January column contains expense information copied from the February column.

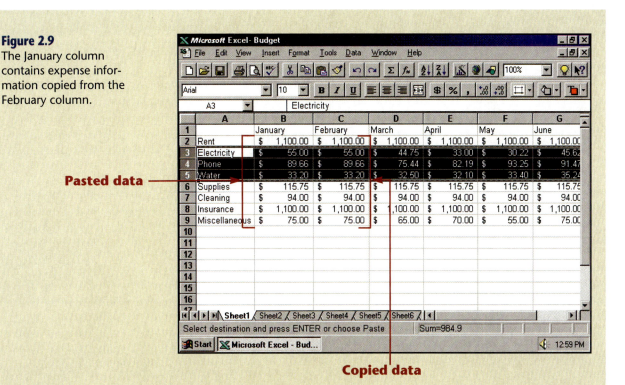

5 **Select cells B2 through G2.**

To estimate your insurance expenses, copy the rent expense information you just selected to the Insurance row.

 6 **Click the Copy button on the Standard toolbar.**

This copies the selected cells the same way as when you use the **E**dit, **C**opy command. The cells' contents are stored in the Clipboard, ready to be pasted.

7 **Click cell B8.**

This selects the location where you want the copied information to appear.

 8 **Click the Paste button on the Standard toolbar.**

The contents of the copied cells are pasted into the new location. Again, notice that the Insurance expense information is exactly the same as the Rent information in row 2. Later in this project, you use formulas to change the amount you just copied. Save your most recent changes and keep the Budget worksheet open to use in the next lesson.

Jargon Watch

When you **copy** or **cut** information in Excel, it moves to the Windows **Clipboard**—a part of memory set aside for storing things that you want to move or copy to another location. The cut or copied information stays in the Clipboard until the next time you cut or copy something. Remember that the Clipboard will only hold one item, although that item can be quite large. Whenever you cut or copy a new piece of information and place it in the Clipboard, it overwrites any information that may already be there. Because information you cut or copy is stored in the Clipboard, you can **paste** the item many times and in many different places.

One thing to keep in mind while you are working in Excel, is the difference between the **Cut**, **Clear**, and **Delete** commands. Cut moves an item from the worksheet to the Clipboard, where it's stored for later use. Clear removes the selected information completely. Delete removes not only the selected information but the cells containing it as well. If you choose the wrong command by mistake, press Ctrl+Z to undo the command, click the Undo button on the Standard toolbar, or choose **E**dit, **U**ndo.

Lesson 6: Moving Information

Your Budget worksheet now has expense information in every cell, but what if you want to look at a certain type of expense separately? For example, perhaps you want to see how your utility expenses compare to the rest of your expenses.

You can use Excel's Cut, Copy, and Paste commands to remove information from one cell and place it in another cell. You can use these commands to move the contents of individual cells and ranges of cells. You don't have to go to each cell, enter the same information, and then erase the information in the old location.

In this lesson, you move the rows containing utility expenses to another part of the worksheet.

To Move Information

1 Select rows 3 through 5 in the Budget worksheet frame.

This highlights the rows of your worksheet that contain utility expenses. These are the rows you will move to another part of the worksheet.

2 From the Edit menu, choose Cut.

The information in rows 3 through 5 moves to the Clipboard (although you can still see it in the worksheet) and a dotted outline appears around the cut text, as shown in Figure 2.10. Rows 3 through 5 remain selected.

Lesson 6: Moving Information

Figure 2.10
Use the **E**dit Cu**t** command to move text from the worksheet to the Windows Clipboard.

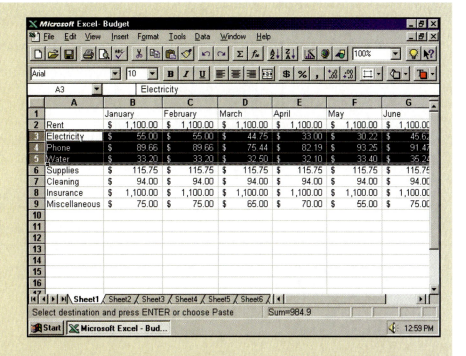

3 **Click cell A10 to select it, and then press the right mouse button.**

Pressing the right mouse button in Excel reveals a shortcut menu, containing several common commands you can use on cells you have selected (see Figure 2.11). Notice that Cut, Copy, and Paste all appear on the shortcut menu.

Figure 2.11
Move the mouse pointer to a select cell or range and click the right mouse button to open a shortcut menu.

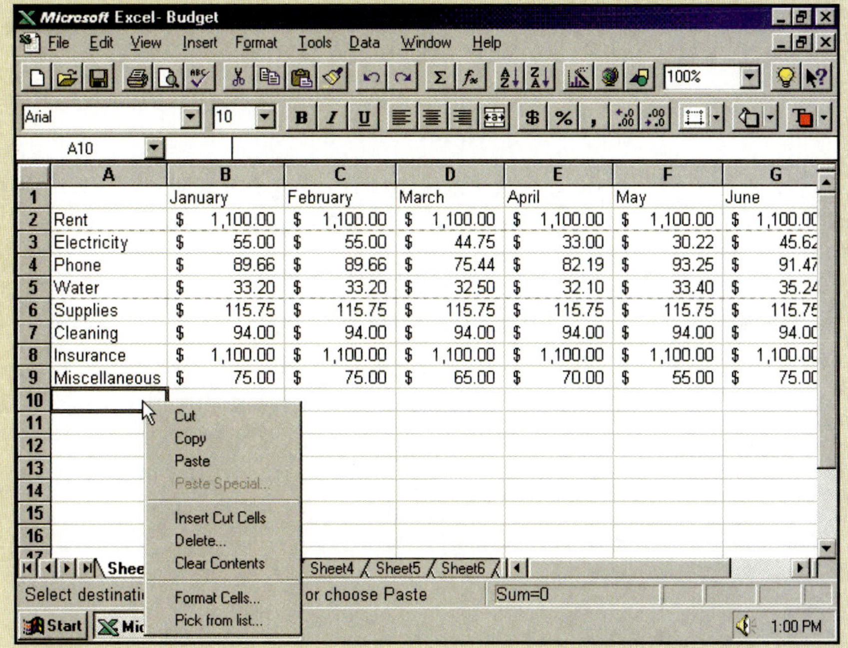

continues

To Move Information (continued)

4 **Choose the Paste command from the shortcut menu.**

The utility expense information is cut from rows 3, 4, and 5 and moved to rows 10, 11, and 12, as shown in Figure 2.12. Now delete the empty rows 3, 4, and 5. Make sure that you move the mouse pointer to the cell or area you have selected before you click the shortcut menu command. Shortcut menu commands happen in the location of the mouse pointer, not necessarily in the current cell.

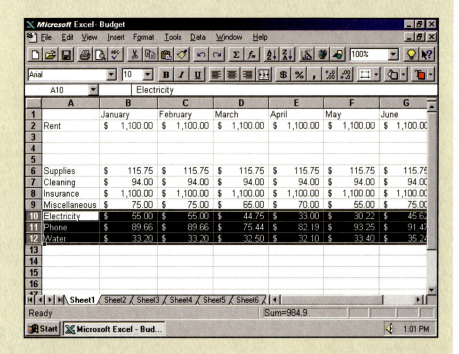

Figure 2.12
Cutting and moving data does not delete existing rows.

5 **Select rows 3 through 5 in the frame of the Budget worksheet.**

6 **Move the mouse pointer to the highlighted area, and then press the right mouse button.**

A shortcut menu appears.

7 **Choose the Delete command from the shortcut menu.**

The shortcut menu disappears and rows 3, 4, and 5 that previously contained the utility bill information are deleted. Your worksheet should now look similar to the one shown in Figure 2.13. Table 2.1 shows some shortcuts for the commonly used Cut, Copy, and Paste commands.

Figure 2.13
The utility information is now in place at the bottom of the worksheet.

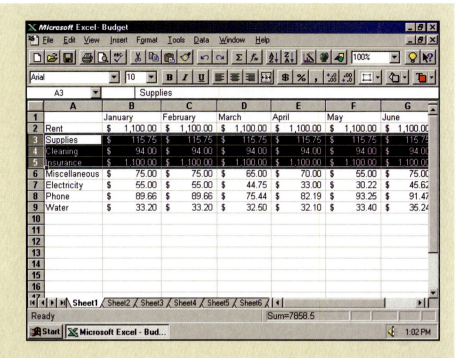

You have now separated the utility expense information by moving it to another part of the worksheet. Save this change and keep the Budget worksheet open to use in the next lesson.

 A handy way of quickly moving one or more cells of data is to select the cells and position the mouse pointer on any border of the cells so that the cell pointer changes to a white arrow. Click and drag the white arrow to the new location. An outline of the cells that you are moving appears as you drag.

When you release the mouse button, the cell contents appear in the new location. If the new location already contains information, a dialog box appears asking whether you want to replace the current information.

Table 2.1 Copying, Cutting, and Pasting		
Command	Tool	Shortcut Key
Edit, **C**ut		Ctrl+x
Edit, **C**opy		Ctrl+c
Edit, **P**aste		Ctrl+v

Lesson 7: Creating Formulas

In this lesson, you learn how to create several kinds of formulas in your Budget worksheet. Formulas use cell addresses, values, and mathematical operators (+ and -, for example) to perform calculations. You can use formulas to add, subtract, multiply, and divide data. Table 2.2 lists the common mathematical operators.

Project 2 Building A Spreadsheet

Table 2.2 Common Mathematical Operators	
Description	Operator
Addition	+ (plus sign)
Subtraction	- (minus sign)
Multiplication	* (asterisks)
Division	/ (forward slash)
Exponentiation	^ (caret)

Formulas are the most valuable part of spreadsheet software such as Microsoft Excel. A worksheet full of data would be of little use without built-in ways to perform calculations on the data.

Once you write a formula using cell addresses, you can change the information in one or more of the cells you used and the formula automatically recalculates a result. The work saved by this automatic calculation is the main attraction of spreadsheet software. Try creating some formulas in your Budget worksheet now.

To Create Formulas

❶ Select cell B5 in the Budget worksheet.

Cell B5 is now the current cell and it is where you want to create your first formula in this example. After looking at the expense worksheet again, you might decide that the estimate of $1100 per month for insurance expenses is too high. To change the insurance bill estimate, divide the amount in half using a formula.

❷ In cell B5, type the formula =b2/2.

Beginning the formula with the = sign tells Excel that you are about to enter a formula. B2 is the cell address of the January rent expense. The / sign is the operator that tells Excel which mathematical operation you want to perform—in this case, division. The formula tells Excel to divide the contents of cell B2 by 2.

❸ Click the Enter button on the Formula bar.

This tells Excel to calculate the formula's result. The result of the formula appears in cell B5, as shown in Figure 2.14. Notice that the formula =B2/2 appears in the Formula bar. Now try creating a formula for February's insurance bill using multiplication rather than division.

Figure 2.14
The result of the formula appears in the cell; the formula itself appears in the Formula bar.

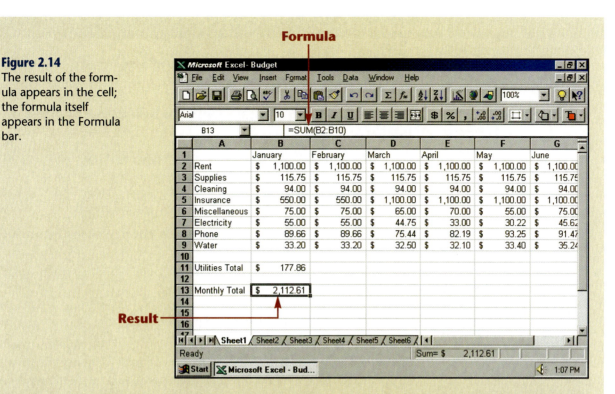

If you have problems...

If your formula results in #NAME? instead of a value, it means you made a mistake entering the formula. You may have typed a cell address that doesn't exist, one of the cells in the formula may have an error, the operator you are using may not exist (for example, \ instead of /), or you may be trying to perform an impossible calculation. Check your formula carefully, correct any mistakes, and try again.

4 **Select cell C5 and enter the formula =c2*.5.**

5 **Click the Enter button on the Formula bar.**

Again, the = tells Excel that you are entering a formula. C2 is the cell address of the February rent expense and * is the operator for multiplication (press ⇧Shift+8 to enter the *). This formula tells Excel to multiply the contents of cell C2 by .5, which is another way to change your estimate of insurance to be 50% of the rent amount.

Next, enter a formula to calculate the total amount spent on utilities in the month of January.

continues

Project 2   Building A Spreadsheet

To Create Formulas (continued)

6 **Select cell A11, type Utilities Total, and press Enter.**

This enters the label in cell A11.

7 **Select cell B11 and click the AutoSum button on the Standard toolbar.**

Clicking the AutoSum button automatically enters a formula for adding the values in the cells immediately above the cell that you have selected—in this case, cells B2:B10. Now change the range in the formula so that it includes only utility information.

8 **Click cell B7 and drag down to cell B9, then release the mouse button.**

Dragging across the cells enters them as the range in the current formula.

9 **Click the Enter button on the Formula bar.**

The values in cells B7 to B9 are totaled, and the result appears in cell B11 (see Figure 2.15). AutoSum is one of Excel's many *functions*. Functions are abbreviated formulas that perform a specific operation on a group of values. You learn more about functions in Project 4.

Function
Functions are built-in formulas, such as AutoSum, that automatically perform calculations.

Figure 2.15
Use the AutoSum button to quickly add values in the cells above or to the left of the selected cell.

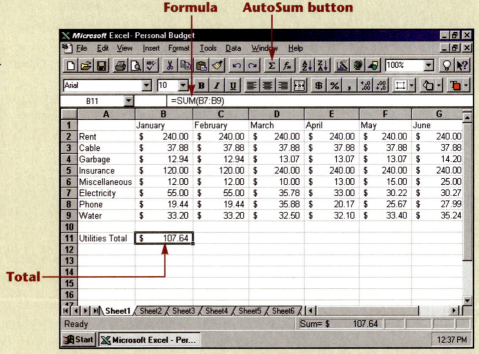

The last formula you need for your Budget worksheet is one that calculates the grand total for each month's expenses.

10 **Select cell A13, type Monthly Total, and press Enter.**

This enters a label; now enter the formula.

Lesson 7: Creating Formulas

11 **Select cell B13 and click the AutoSum button on the Standard toolbar.**

Again, clicking the AutoSum button totals the cells above the cell you selected. The formula =SUM(B2:B12) appears in the Formula bar. In this case, however, you want to find the total of all the month's expenses, not including the total for utilities. The formula and amount in cell B13 don't give you that total. To correct the formula, change the cell range of the AutoSum function in the Formula bar.

12 **Move the mouse pointer to the Formula bar and position the I-beam cursor between B12 and the).**

When you position the mouse pointer in the Formula bar, it becomes an I-beam shape to indicate where information you enter will appear in the Formula bar.

13 **Press (Backspace) once to delete the 2, and then type 0.**

This changes the cell range to the one you want to use in the formula.

14 **Click the Enter button to calculate the formula and keep cell B13 the active cell.**

The formula =SUM(B2:B10) appears in the Formula bar, and your total expenses for January, $2,112.61, appears in cell B13 (see Figure 2.16).

You have now entered all the formulas you need in your Budget worksheet. Save your changes and leave the Budget worksheet open. You learn to copy these formulas to the rest of the worksheet in the next lesson.

Figure 2.16
The result of the formula in the Formula bar appears in cell B13.

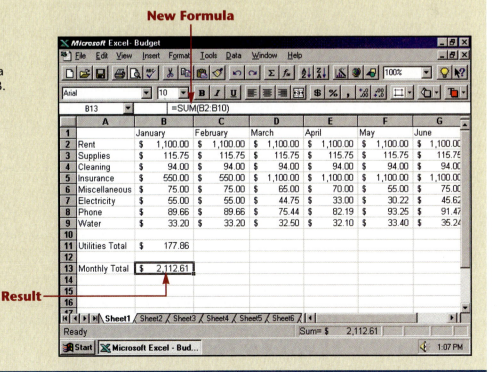

The parentheses in a formula tell Excel which order to use when performing calculations. For example, if you want to add two numbers and then divide them by 2, you use the formula =(A12+B12)/2. The part of the formula in parentheses takes precedence over the other parts of the formula.

If you don't use parentheses in a formula, Excel sets precedence in the following way: Exponentiation first, multiplication second, and addition and subtraction third. So, with a formula such as =B12+C12/A10, Excel first divides C12 by A10. Then Excel adds the resulting number to B12. If you want to add the first two cells and then divide, use the formula =(B12+C12)/A10.

You can use Excel's AutoCalculate feature to find out the result of a calculation without actually entering a formula. Simply select the cell or range of cells you want to total and look at the AutoCalculate button on the Status bar. By default, Excel uses the Sum function. To select a different function, right-click the AutoCalculate button and choose the function you want to use.

Lesson 8: Copying Formulas

After you create a formula, you can copy it to other cells or worksheets to help speed up your work. When you copy a formula from one cell to another, Excel automatically references the appropriate column or row in the formula.

Now finish building the Budget worksheet by copying formulas.

To Copy Formulas

1 **Select cell C5 in the Budget worksheet.**

Cell C5 contains the formula =C2*.5, which is the formula you want to copy to the rest of the cells in the Insurance row.

2 **With the mouse pointer in cell C5, press the right mouse button.**

A shortcut menu appears, which you can use to copy the formula.

3 **Click the Copy command on the shortcut menu.**

The shortcut menu disappears and the formula is copied to the Clipboard. Remember, you are copying the formula, not the value in the cell.

4 **Select cells D5 through G5.**

This is the range where you want to copy the formula.

5 **Move the mouse pointer to the active cell, D5, open the shortcut menu, and choose the Paste command.**

Excel inserts the copied formula into the selected cells, as shown in Figure 2.17. Again, make sure that you move the mouse pointer to the active cell before you issue the Paste command. Notice that the

Lesson 8: Copying Formulas

formulas copied into each cell are *relative* to the new cells. For example, the formula in cell D5, =D2* 0.5, refers to rent information for the month of March rather than the month of February. The results of the new formulas are displayed in each cell.

Figure 2.17
The formula totals the cells' contents and enters the result in the correct cells.

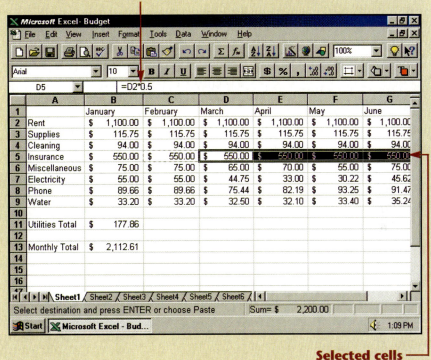

Now copy the formula for the utilities total to the rest of the worksheet.

❻ Select cell B11 and click the Copy button on the Standard toolbar.

You can use the toolbar buttons or menu commands to copy and paste formulas the same way you copy text or numbers.

❼ Select cells C11 through G11.

You want to copy the formula into these cells.

❽ Click the Paste button on the toolbar.

Excel copies the SUM formula to add the utilities total in each month to the cells you selected. Again, notice that the cell references in the formulas refer to the appropriate month in each case. Now copy the formula for the monthly total to complete the worksheet.

❾ Select cell B13 and move the mouse pointer to the lower-right corner of the cell so that the pointer changes to a black cross.

continues

To Copy Formulas (continued)

You also can use AutoFill to copy the formula to the rest of the cells in the row. When the mouse pointer changes to the black cross, you can select the other cells that need the formula.

❿ Press the left mouse button and drag right to select cells C13 to G13.

This selects the range you want to fill. When you release the mouse button in cell G13, Excel fills the range with the formula and displays the results of the formula in each cell. Again, the formulas are relative.

You have now completed the Budget worksheet. It should look similar to the one in Figure 2.18. Save your changes. If requested by your instructor, print two copies. Then close the Budget file.

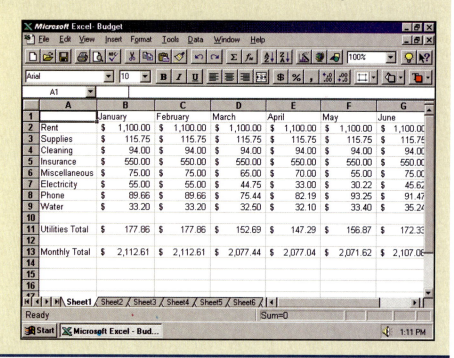

Figure 2.18
The completed Budget worksheet.

Jargon Watch

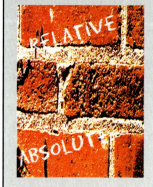

When you copy a formula, Excel assumes that the formula is **relative**. The cell addresses in the formula change when you copy the formula to another part of the worksheet. If, for example, you copy the formula =SUM(A2:A9) from cell A10 to cell B10, the formula automatically changes to =SUM(B2:B9). No matter where you copy the formula, it updates to reflect the cells that are relative to it.

If you want to copy a formula to another cell but have it return exactly the same result, you must specify **absolute** cell references. To specify absolute references, you add a $ (dollar sign) before a column or row part of the formula. For example, to copy =SUM(A2:A9) and make sure that the resulting value is the same, you change the formula to =SUM($A$2:$A$9).

Project Summary

To	Do This
Open an existing file	Choose **F**ile, **O**pen, choose the file name in the Open dialog box, then choose Open.
Save a file with a new name	Choose **F**ile, Save **A**s, type a new name in the File **n**ame text box, then choose **S**ave.
Select a cell	Click the cell you want to select.
Select a range of cells	Drag from the first cell to the last cell.
AutoFill a range of cells	Select the cell containing the first entry in the series, then drag across the range you want to fill.
Insert rows or columns	Select the row(s) or column(s), then choose **I**nsert, **R**ows or Insert, **C**olumns.
Delete rows or columns	Select the row(s) or column(s), then choose **E**dit, **D**elete.
Copy cells	Select the cell(s) to copy, then click the Copy button on the toolbar.
Move cells	Select the cell(s) to move, then click the Cut button on the toolbar.
Paste cells	Copy or cut the cell(s), select the new location, then click the Paste button on the toolbar.
Automatically total a range of cells	Select a blank cell at the bottom or to the right of a range of cells, then click the AutoSum button on the toolbar, then click the Enter button on the Formula bar.

Applying Your Skills

Take a few minutes to practice the skills you have learned in this project by completing the following exercises.

Calculating Travel Expenses

Now that you are familiar with Excel functions, you can make use of them to calculate travel expenses. Using the sample file Proj0202, complete the travel expense worksheet by creating formulas and copying them to the appropriate cells.

To Calculate Travel Expenses

1. Start Excel, open the file Proj0202, and save it as **Travel Expenses**.
2. In the Travel workbook file, create the formulas to total the number of miles per month for January, February, and March on the left in cells C12, C13, and C14, respectively.

3. Copy those formulas to the totals columns for April, May, and June on the right, in cells G12, G13, and G14, respectively.

4. Create formulas to calculate the total miles for each quarter of the year in cells C15 and G15.

5. Using a blank cell in the worksheet, enter the cell label **Reimbursement.**

6. In the cell immediately to the right of the Reimbursement label, create a formula multiplying the total miles for all six months by 28 cents per mile.

7. Save your work. If requested by your instructor, print two copies. Then close the Travel file.

Calculating Regional Sales Percentages

For Sound Byte Music, use the information provided to create a worksheet calculating the percent of total sales that come from regional sales.

To Calculate Regional Sales Percentages

1. Using the default worksheet, enter the following data in columns A through D.

	A	B	C	D	E
1		Regional Sales in Thousands			
2		Region	Sales	% of Total	
3		South	100		
4		North	90		
5		East	187		
6		West	78		
7		Total Sales			

2. Total the sales and insert the value in cell C7.

3. In cell D3, type the formula **=C3/C7**.

4. Copy the formula into cells D4, D5, and D6.

5. Notice the error messages appearing in column D. Referring to the formula bar, note the formulas that Excel is using. Observe that because the formula does not include a mixed cell reference, the worksheet is of little value.

6. Correct the formula in cell D4 and copy the revised formula into the other related cells. *Hint:* The revised formula should be =C4/C$7.

7. Save the file as **Regional Sales.**

8. If requested by your instructor, print two copies of the worksheet. Then close it.

Expanding the Paper Costs Worksheet

In this exercise, follow the steps below to expand the Paper Costs worksheet you first created in Project 1.

To Expand the Paper Costs Worksheet

1. Open the file Proj0203 and save it as **More Paper Costs**.
2. Insert a new row 5 and label it for fax paper.
3. Enter **500** as the amount you spent on fax paper.
4. Make sure the function in cell B7 is correct for adding the values in cells B1:B6.
5. Rearrange the rows so that the cost of letterhead paper and the cost of envelopes are at the top of the worksheet. Remember that if you paste data over existing data, the existing data is erased (*Hint*: insert the necessary row(s) before pasting.)
6. Save the worksheet. If requested by your instructor, print two copies. Then close it.

Changing a Course List

You can use the editing techniques you learned in this project to make changes to the course list worksheet you created in Project 1.

To Change the Course List

1. Open the file Proj0204 and save it as **Change Courses**.
2. Delete the Government course in row 7, then insert a new course: Astronomy 101, for the winter semester, on Tuesdays and Thursdays at 1. The professor is O'Ryan, and it will not count toward your major.
3. Rearrange the courses by semester, so you can easily see if any overlap.
4. Save the worksheet. If requested by your instructor, print two copies. Then close it.

Checking Your Skills

True/False

For each of the following, check *T* or *F* to indicate whether the statement is true or false.

_T _F **1.** You use the **F**ile, **O**pen command to retrieve a file that has been previously saved.

_T _F **2.** Select the entire worksheet by clicking the sheet tab.

_T _F **3.** To insert two rows, select two rows and then choose the **E**dit, **I**nsert command.

__T __F 4. When you copy a formula, Excel assumes it is relative unless you add the dollar sign before each column or row part.

__T __F 5. Pressing F9 is a shortcut for deleting selected rows.

Multiple Choice

Circle the letter of the correct answer for each of the following.

1. Which of the following is false when working with AutoFill?
   a. When you select cells already containing data to fill by example, it means that Excel overwrites the data in the cells.
   b. If Excel can't recognize a pattern from the first two selected cells it uses only the data in the first cell.
   c. If you enter April in a cell and fill the next two cells by example, Excel enters May and June in the next two cells.
   d. You can fill only days, months, and dates by example.

2. Which of the following is *not* a valid formula?
   a. B3+B4+B5
   b. =SUM(B2:B9)
   c. =B12+C12/A10
   d. =(B12+C12)/A10

3. Which of the following *cannot* be pasted?
   a. data that has been cut
   b. data that has been cleared
   c. data that has been copied
   d. data that you just pasted

4. Which of the following does *not* represent how to copy a formula?
   a. click the Copy button on the toolbar
   b. choose the **E**dit, **C**opy command
   c. drag the formula to the cell you want to copy it to
   d. use the SpeedFill button on the toolbar

5. Which of the following is *not* a mathematical operator?
   a. + (plus sign)
   b. ^ (caret)
   c. @ (at sign)
   d. - (hyphen)

Checking Your Skills

Completion

In the blank provided, write the correct answer for each of the following statements.

1. To retrieve a file that has already been saved, you open the **F**ile menu and choose the _____ command.

2. To select several cells in succession, you _____ the mouse over the cells.

3. When using AutoFill, the next in sequence to Quarter 1 is _____.

4. The dollar sign ($) represents parts of the formula that are _____.

5. Select, or _____, a cell when you want to cut or copy the cell contents.

Project 3

Improving the Appearance of a Worksheet

Formatting a Budget

In this project, you learn how to
- ➤ Use Fonts and Attributes
- ➤ Align Text and Numbers
- ➤ Change Column Width
- ➤ Format Numbers
- ➤ Add Borders and Shading
- ➤ Use the AutoFormat Feature
- ➤ Use the Spelling Checker

Project 3: Improving the Appearance of a Worksheet

Why Would I Do This?

Having completed the first two projects of *Excel for Windows 95 Essentials*, you now know how to build your own Excel worksheet. The office expense worksheet you created contains formulas and functions that provide you with useful information about your expenses.

Formatting
Applying attributes to text and data to change the appearance of a worksheet or to call attention to certain information.

After you create a basic worksheet, however, you may want to improve its appearance by *formatting* it, so that it is more readable and attractive. In this project, you learn how to improve the appearance of worksheets by using many of Excel's formatting features. You also learn how to check for spelling errors in a worksheet.

Lesson 1: Using Fonts and Attributes

Font
The typeface, type size, and type attributes of text or numbers.

You can dramatically improve the appearance of your worksheet by using different fonts. A *font* is the typeface, type size, and type attributes that you apply to text and numbers. Excel and Windows 95 supply a variety of typefaces and sizes that you can use. Try using some different fonts and attributes in a worksheet now.

To Use Fonts and Attributes

1 Open the Proj0301 worksheet and save it as **Budget2**.

2 Select cells B2 through H2 in the Budget2 file.

This selects the column headings in the Budget2 worksheet—the first text you want to change. In Excel, you can change the formatting of a single selected cell, or of a range of selected cells.

3 Open the **Format** menu, and choose the **Cells** command.

Excel displays the Format Cells dialog box, where you can change a number of formatting settings for the cells you have selected.

4 Click the **Font** tab.

The Font options of the Format Cells dialog box appear, as shown in Figure 3.1.

5 In the **Font** list box, select **Times New Roman**.

This selects the typeface you want to apply to the selected cells in this example. You may have to use the scroll arrows to scroll down through the list of fonts to get to Times New Roman. Excel displays a sample of the typeface in the Preview box.

Lesson 1: Using Fonts and Attributes

Figure 3.1
The Font options of the Format cells dialog box.

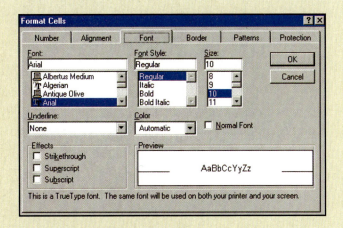

6 **In the Size list box, select 14.**

Again, you may need to scroll down the list to find 14. The size of the type in the selected cells, which contain the column labels of the worksheet, is increased. Excel shows how the new type will look in the Preview box.

7 **In the Font Style box, select Bold.**

The text in the Preview box now appears in bold.

8 **Choose OK.**

All the month headings now appear in the new font and attributes, as shown in Figure 3.2. Notice that the row height automatically adjusts to accommodate the new type size. Now apply the same type style to the expense labels in column A.

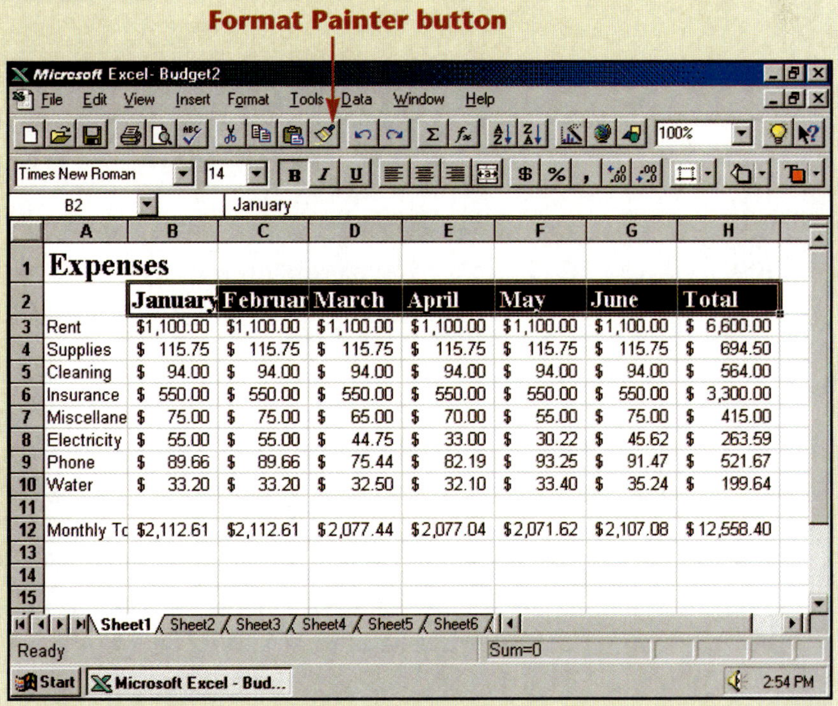

Figure 3.2
The month headings in a new typeface and type size.

continues

Project 3: Improving the Appearance of a Worksheet

To Use Fonts and Attributes (continued)

9 **Click the Format Painter button on the Standard toolbar.**

The mouse pointer changes to a white cross with a paintbrush. This shows that you can now apply the formatting from the cell or cells you have selected to other cells in the worksheet.

10 **Click cell A3 and drag the mouse pointer down to cell A12, then release the mouse button.**

This selects the range A3 through A12. Notice that the status bar reminds you what to do next (see Figure 3.3). When you release the mouse button, the formatting from the column heading is applied to the range you selected.

Figure 3.3
Formatting is copied to the selected range of cells.

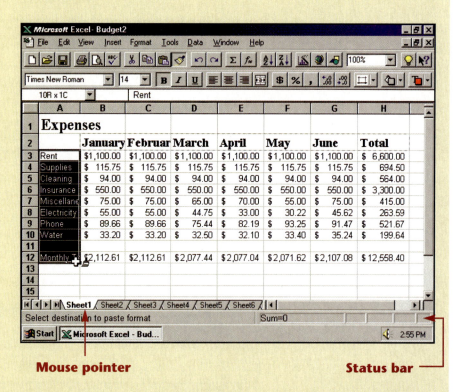

Mouse pointer   Status bar

Save your work and leave the Budget2 workbook open for the next lesson, where you learn how to change the alignment of information in your worksheet.

In Excel, you can use the buttons on the Formatting toolbar to quickly change the formatting of selected cells. If you want to change the font in only part of your worksheet, select the cells you want to change, then click the drop-down arrow to the right of the Font box and select the font you want to use.

You can also change type size by clicking the drop-down arrow to the right of the Font size box and choosing a new size.

To change attributes, simply click the Bold, Italic, or Underline button on the Formatting toolbar, or use the following keyboard shortcuts: Bold—Ctrl+B, Italic—Ctrl+I, Underline—Ctrl+U.

Lesson 2: Aligning Text and Numbers

When you enter information into a cell, numbers, dates, and times automatically align with the right side of the cell. Labels, which are usually text, align with the left side of the cell. You can change the alignment of information at any time. For instance, you may want to fine-tune the appearance of column headings by centering all the information in the column. You can also align data across several columns in one step. Now try aligning data in Budget2.

To Align Text and Numbers

❶ Select cells B2 through H2 in the Budget2 worksheet.

This selects all the cells you want to change. Notice that the column labels are left-aligned. Improve the appearance of the worksheet by centering the data in the selected cells.

❷ Click the Center button on the Formatting toolbar.

The text in the selected columns centers within each column, as shown in Figure 3.4. Now center the title of the worksheet over the entire worksheet.

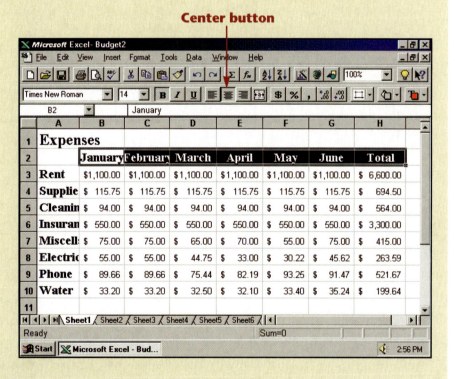

Figure 3.4
The contents of the selected cells are now centered.

❸ Select the range A1 through H1.

This is the range of cells in which you want to center the worksheet title. Cell A1 contains the worksheet title.

continues

Project 3: Improving the Appearance of a Worksheet

To Align Text and Numbers (continued)

 ❹ **Click the Center Across Columns button on the Formatting toolbar.**

The text centers across the selected cells, as shown in Figure 3.5. Even though the worksheet title is centered across the worksheet, it is still located in cell A1. If you want to select the text for further formatting or editing, you must select cell A1.

Figure 3.5
Text is centered across the selected cells.

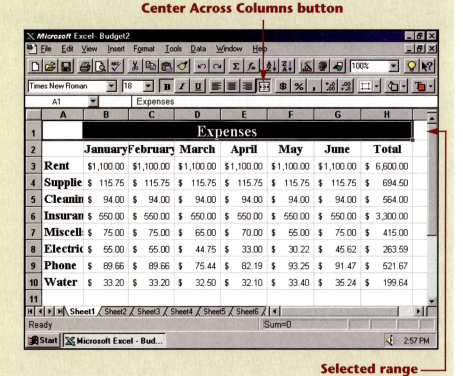

Save your work and keep Budget2 open for the next lesson, where you adjust column width.

 The Alignment tab of the Format Cells dialog box contains orientation options. You can display text vertically or horizontally in a cell. To display the Format Cells dialog box, select the cells you want to format, move the mouse pointer to the highlighted range, click the right mouse button, and then choose Format Cells from the shortcut menu.

The Alignment tab also includes a Wrap Text option. Use this option when you want to enter more than one line of text within a cell. As you type, the text automatically wraps to the next line in the cell.

Figure 3.6 shows the various orientations and the word wrap option.

Figure 3.6
The Format Cells dialog box.

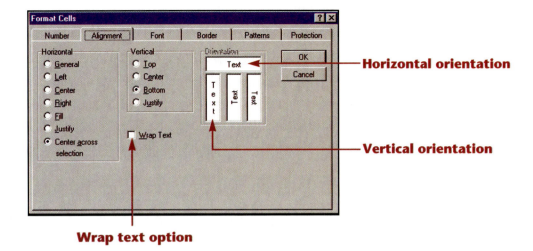

Lesson 3: Changing Column Width

As you may have noticed, several of the column and row labels of the Budget2 worksheet don't fit in the default column width. Although row heights adjust automatically when you change fonts, column widths do not. To make your information fit, you can increase or decrease column widths; you can also change row height, if necessary. Change the width of a column in your worksheet now.

To Change Column Width

1 In the Budget2 worksheet frame, move the mouse pointer to the line to the right of column letter A.

The mouse pointer changes to a double-headed black arrow, as shown in Figure 3.7. Column A is the column you want to change. Notice that several of the expense labels in column A are covered by information in column B.

continues

To Change Column Width (continued)

Figure 3.7
The mouse pointer changes to let you adjust the column width.

Double-headed arrow

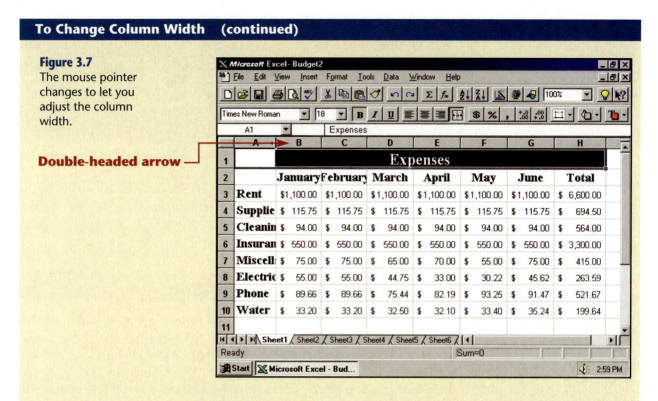

2 **Double-click the left mouse button.**

When you double-click the line between column letters A and B, the width of column A automatically adjusts to fit the longest entry. Now adjust the widths of columns B and C.

3 **Double-click the line to the right of column B, and then double-click the line to the right of column C.**

These actions adjust the widths of columns B and C to fit the longest entry. Your worksheet should now look like Figure 3.8.

Figure 3.8
The adjusted column width fits the longest entry in the column.

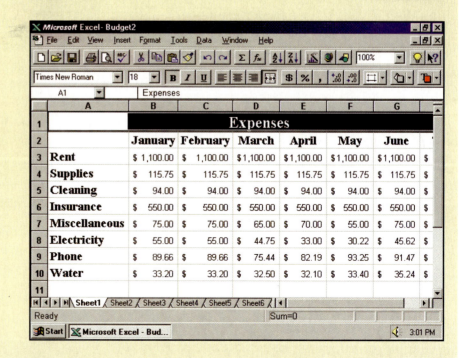

Lesson 4: Formatting Numbers

You have now completed formatting your Budget2 worksheet. Save your work and close Budget2. If requested by your instructor, print two copies before closing the file. You use a different worksheet to complete the lessons in the rest of the project.

When a label doesn't fit in the width of a column, the label appears to be cut off or hidden by the next cell. If a number doesn't fit in the width of a column, a series of ###### appears in the cell.

Rather than double-clicking the column or row border to force Excel to automatically reset the width or height, you can experiment with widths and heights by using the double-arrow pointer to drag the column and row borders in the worksheet frame. Move the mouse pointer to the border; when the double-arrow appears, click and drag the border until you're satisfied with the new width or height.

To enter a precise column width, choose the F**o**rmat, **C**olumn, Column **W**idth command, then enter the width (in number of characters) in the **C**olumn Width text box and choose OK. To enter a precise row height, choose the F**o**rmat, **R**ow, Row H**e**ight command, then enter the height (in points) in the Row Height text box and choose OK. The default row height is 12.75 points.

If you want to reset the column width to the original setting, choose the F**o**rmat, **C**olumn, **S**tandard Width command, make sure that 8.43 is entered in the Standard Column Width box, and then choose OK.

To undo the most recent formatting changes, click the Undo button, or choose **E**dit, **U**ndo.

You can select several cells, columns, or rows simultaneously to apply any formatting changes to all the selected parts of the worksheet.

Lesson 4: Formatting Numbers

When you enter a number or a formula into a cell, the entry may not appear as you hoped it would. You might enter 5, for example, but want it to look like $5.00. When you want to change the appearance of a number, you format it.

In Excel, you can format numbers in many ways. You will probably format numbers most often as currency, percentages, a date, or a time. Remember that when you apply any kind of formatting, you apply it to the worksheet cell, not to the information itself. This means that if you change the information, the formatting still applies.

In the remainder of this project, you learn how to improve the appearance of a sample worksheet that tracks monthly sales for four sales representatives. Try formatting the numbers in this worksheet now.

Project 3: Improving the Appearance of a Worksheet

To Format Numbers

1 Open the Proj0302 worksheet and save it as **Sales**.

2 Select cells C4 through F8 of the Sales worksheet.

These are the cells you want to format.

3 Click the Currency Style button on the Formatting toolbar.

This changes the selected cells to display the default currency format, as shown in Figure 3.9.

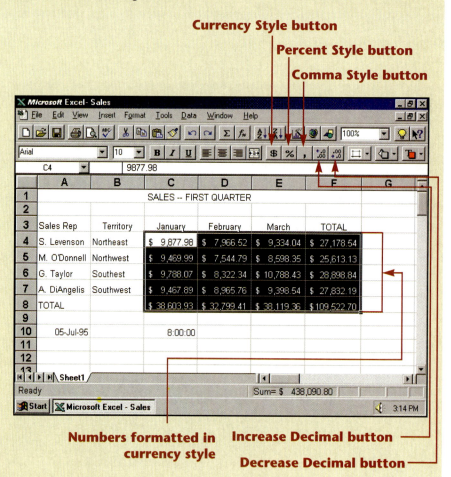

Figure 3.9
Quickly select a format for the cell(s) using the buttons on the Formatting toolbar.

4 Click the Decrease Decimal button twice.

This tells Excel to display zero decimal places. Because no decimal places are displayed, Excel rounds the values that are displayed to fit this format (see Figure 3.10). However, the actual values will be used in any calculations.

Lesson 4: Formatting Numbers

Figure 3.10
Use the Decrease Decimal button to decrease the number of decimal places displayed.

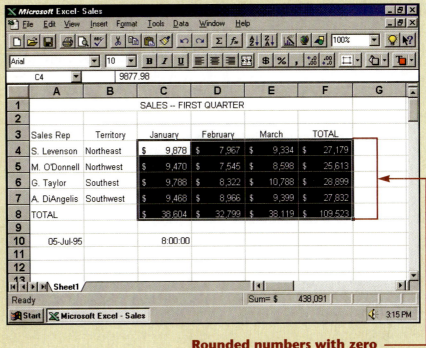

Rounded numbers with zero decimal places

5 **Click cell A10.**

In this example, you decide that you want to change the way the date is displayed in the worksheet.

6 **Move the mouse pointer to cell A10, click the right mouse button and choose Format Cells from the shortcut menu.**

Excel opens the Format Cells dialog box. (Recall that you can also open this dialog box from the Format menu.)

7 **Click the Number tab in the Format Cells dialog box.**

8 **Select the 3/4/95 format from the Type list box (see Figure 3.11).**

Notice that the Sample line shows the date in cell A10 in the format you selected.

continues

To Format Numbers (continued)

Figure 3.11
Apply a date format to the selected cell.

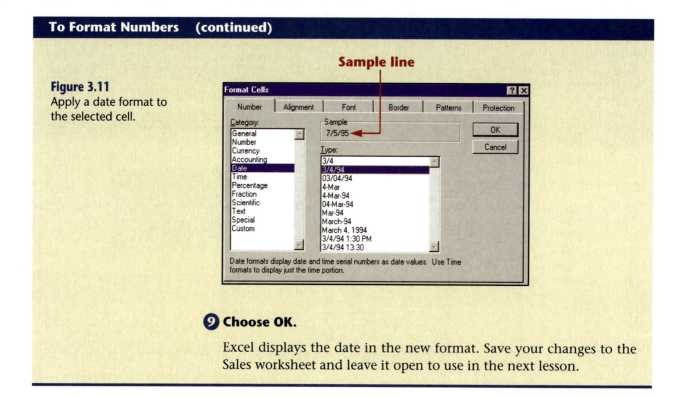

9 Choose OK.

Excel displays the date in the new format. Save your changes to the Sales worksheet and leave it open to use in the next lesson.

Lesson 5: Adding Borders and Shading

After formatting the numbers in your Sales worksheet, you may want to highlight certain cells to make them stand out. You can do this by changing the font or attributes of the numbers, as you learned earlier in this project, or you can change the appearance of the cell itself.

You can add a border or shading to a cell or range of cells to emphasize important information. For example, you may want to highlight the highest sales for a month and the grand total.

Now try adding borders and shading to the Sales worksheet.

To Add Borders and Shading

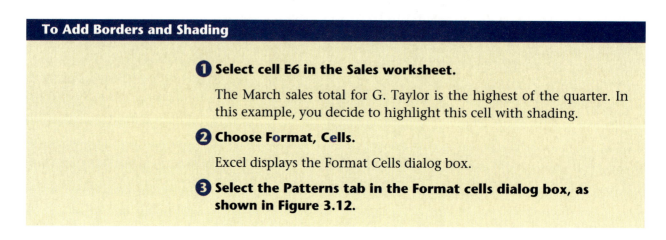

1 Select cell E6 in the Sales worksheet.

The March sales total for G. Taylor is the highest of the quarter. In this example, you decide to highlight this cell with shading.

2 Choose Format, Cells.

Excel displays the Format Cells dialog box.

3 Select the Patterns tab in the Format cells dialog box, as shown in Figure 3.12.

Lesson 5: Adding Borders and Shading

Figure 3.12
The Patterns options in the Format Cells dialog box.

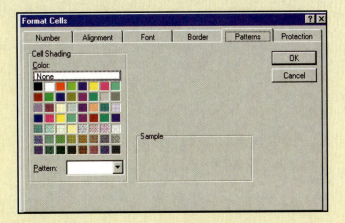

4 **Click the Pattern drop-down arrow.**

A palette of shading patterns appears, as shown in Figure 3.13. Clicking any of these patterns displays a sample in the Sample area.

Figure 3.13
The Pattern palette in the Format Cells dialog box.

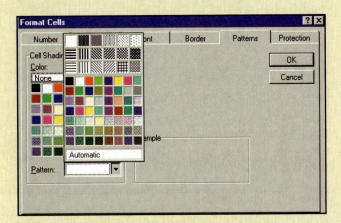

5 **Click the pattern at the far right in the first row of the palette.**

This selects a light, dotted pattern. This simple pattern will ensure that you can easily read the number in the worksheet cell.

6 **Choose OK.**

This confirms the change. You see the shading in cell E6 on-screen. Next, add a border to outline the totals for each sales representative.

7 **Select cells F3 through F8.**

This selects the range you want to highlight.

8 **Click the right mouse button and choose Format Cells from the shortcut menu.**

As you can see, you can also open the Format Cells dialog box from the shortcut menu. Remember to position the mouse pointer on the range you want to affect with the shortcut menu.

continues

Project 3: Improving the Appearance of a Worksheet

To Add Borders and Shading   (continued)

9 **Click the Border tab to display the border options, then click in the Outline box of the Border area.**

A single thin line appears in the Outline box. This selects the Outline option, which applies a border to the cell or range of cells you select. Now select a style of border to apply.

10 **Select the thick line at the bottom of the first column of the Style area.**

This selects a thick border that will stand out clearly from the rest of the worksheet (see Figure 3.14).

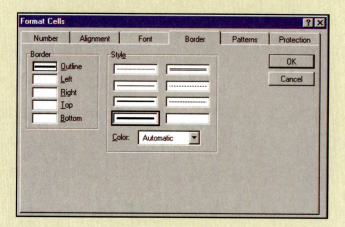

Figure 3.14
The Border options in the Format Cells dialog box.

11 **Choose OK.**

This tells Excel to outline the edges of the range with a single line. Click any other cell to deselect the range so that you can see the outline better. Your worksheet should now look like the one shown in Figure 3.15. Save your changes to the Sales worksheet and leave it open to use in the next lesson.

Lesson 6: Using the AutoFormat Feature

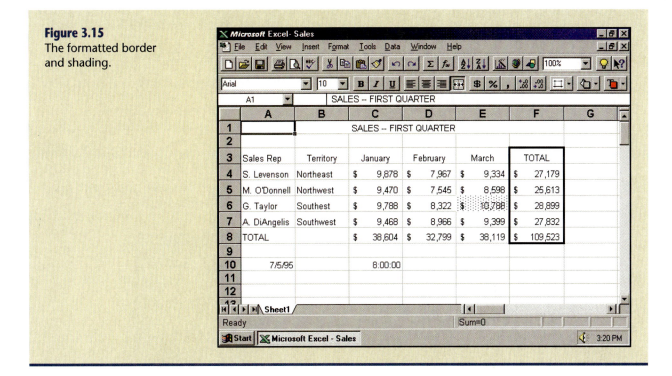

Figure 3.15
The formatted border and shading.

One of the most entertaining things about working with Windows 95 applications is being able to use a variety of colors. Excel allows you to personalize your work with color through the Format Cells dialog box.

Unfortunately, colored letters on a colored background may be clear and attractive on-screen, but hard to read in printed form. Keep in mind that you need to be connected to a color printer to be able to print color worksheets. Without a color printer, colors may turn out to be muddy gray on paper, and all but the simplest patterns may make information on the worksheet hard to read.

Have fun experimenting with the colors and patterns in the Format Cells dialog box, but keep the formatting simple on worksheets that you need to print.

Lesson 6: Using the AutoFormat Feature

If you don't want to spend a lot of time formatting a worksheet, or if you want to rely on someone else's flair for design, you can use Excel's AutoFormat feature. The AutoFormat feature contains several table formats that you can apply to selected cells in your worksheet.

Each format contains various alignment, number format, color, and pattern settings to help you create professional-looking worksheets. Generally, you apply one format at a time to a selected cell or range of cells. With a table format you can apply a collection of formats supplied by Excel all at once.

Now try using one of the table formats in the AutoFormat feature to improve the appearance of the Sales worksheet.

To Use AutoFormat

1 **Select cells A1 through F8 in the Sales worksheet.**

This highlights the entire worksheet, except the date and time. Now apply the new format to this range.

2 **Choose Format, AutoFormat.**

Excel displays the AutoFormat dialog box (see Figure 3.16). A list of table formats and a Sample area appear in the dialog box. The Simple table format is currently selected. You can click other table formats to see what they look like in the Sample area.

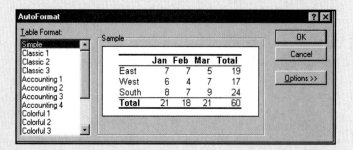

Figure 3.16
The AutoFormat dialog box.

3 **Scroll down the Table format list box and select the 3D Effects 1 format.**

This selects the 3D Effects 1 table format.

4 **Choose OK.**

Excel changes the selected cells to the new format, as shown in Figure 3.16. Click any cell to deselect the range so that you can see the formatting clearly. Notice that the previous formatting in the Sales worksheet has been replaced by the new format. If you plan to use the AutoFormat feature, apply AutoFormat before adding other formatting.

5 **Select column A.**

You need to adjust the width of column A. The new table format changed the width of the column so that not all the entries fit in the column width.

6 **Click the right mouse button and choose Column Width from the shortcut menu.**

The Column Width dialog box opens.

7 **Type 13 in the Column Width text box and choose OK.**

This changes the width of the column so that you can read all the data. Click anywhere outside the selected cells so that you can better see the formatted worksheet, as shown in Figure 3.17. Save your changes to the Sales worksheet and leave it open for the next lesson, where you learn how to check for spelling errors.

Lesson 7: Using the Spelling Checker

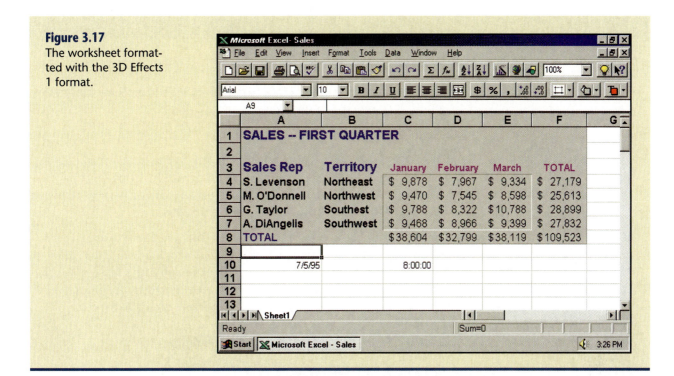

Figure 3.17
The worksheet formatted with the 3D Effects 1 format.

If you have problems...

The table formats in the AutoFormat dialog box can drastically change the appearance of your worksheet. If you don't like the results after closing the AutoFormat dialog box, choose the **E**dit, **U**ndo command before you take any other action. Alternatively, you can continue making formatting changes to the worksheet.

Lesson 7: Using the Spelling Checker

When presenting a worksheet, you should make sure that no misspelled words are in the document. You can use the Excel Spelling Checker to rapidly find and highlight any misspelled words in a worksheet.

You have the option of correcting or bypassing words that the Spelling Checker highlights. To personalize the program, you can add proper names, cities, and technical terms to the spelling dictionary.

Now use the Spelling Checker on your Sales worksheet to correct any spelling errors.

To Use the Spelling Checker

❶ Select cell A1.

This makes A1 the current cell so that Excel will begin checking the spelling at the top of the worksheet.

❷ Choose Tools, Spelling.

The Spelling Checker starts to search the worksheet for spelling errors. When it finds a word it doesn't recognize, it stops, highlights the word in the text, and opens the Spelling dialog box where it makes suggestions on how you can correct the word.

In this example, the Spelling Checker stops on the word Levenson and displays the Spelling dialog box, as shown in Figure 3.18. Levenson is a proper name that is not in the Spelling Checker's dictionary. You can choose to **A**dd it to the dictionary, **I**gnore All occurrences of the word, or **I**gnore this occurrence of the word.

Figure 3.18
The Spelling dialog box.

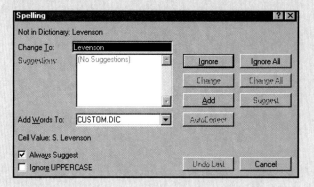

❸ Choose Ignore.

Excel leaves the name intact and moves on to highlight the next word it believes is misspelled—O'Donnell, another proper name. If you think you will include the name in many workbooks, you should add it to the dictionary. Then if you misspell it in the future, you can count on the Spelling Checker to correct it.

❹ Choose Add.

Excel adds the name to the dictionary, and moves on to highlight the next word it believes is misspelled—Southest. In this case, Excel suggests a list of alternative spellings, as shown in Figure 3.19. The correct spelling—Southeast—is highlighted at the top of the list. You can select a different alternative, or, if the correct spelling isn't listed, you can type it in the Change **T**o text box.

Lesson 7: Using the Spelling Checker

Figure 3.19
Words not found in the dictionary are questioned by the Spelling Checker.

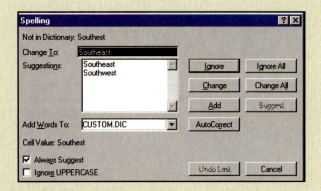

5 **Choose Change.**

Excel replaces the incorrect spelling with the correct spelling and continues to check the spelling of the rest of the worksheet. Once again, when the Spelling Checker comes across a proper name—DiAngelis—it stops. In this case, however, the name is similar to some words that are in the dictionary, so Excel offers a list of alternatives.

6 **Choose Ignore.**

The Spelling Checker doesn't find any more misspelled words and displays the message Finished spell checking entire sheet.

7 **Choose OK.**

This confirms that the spelling check is complete. The word Southeast now appears correctly spelled in the Sales worksheet. Table 3.1 describes the options in the Spelling dialog box.

Save your work and close the worksheet. If you have completed your session on the computer, exit Excel and Windows 95 before turning off the computer. Otherwise, continue with the "Applying Your Skills" section at the end of this project.

Table 3.1	Spelling Button Options
Option	Description
Change **A**ll	Substitutes all occurrences of the questionable word with the word in the Change **T**o text box.
Change	Substitutes only this one occurrence with the word in the Change **T**o text box.
Ignore All	Ignores all occurrences of the questionable word in this worksheet.
Ignore	Ignores only this one occurrence of the questionable word.
Add	Adds the word to the dictionary.

> **If you have problems...**
>
> If the Spelling dialog box doesn't suggest alternatives to a misspelled word, you need to select the Always Suggest check box in the Spelling dialog box.

To quickly start the Spelling Checker, click the Spelling button on the Standard toolbar, or press F7.

Excel comes with an AutoCorrect feature that automatically corrects common spelling errors. For example, if you type "adn", Excel will automatically replace it with "and." To see the list of words Excel will automatically correct, choose **T**ools, **A**utoCorrect. To add your own personal spelling bugaboos to AutoCorrect, enter the incorrect spelling in the **R**eplace text box and the correct spelling in the **W**ith text box, choose **A**dd, then choose OK.

Project Summary

To	Do This
Change fonts, font sizes, or font attributes	Select the cells to format, choose **F**ormat, **C**ells, click the Font tab, make selections, and choose OK.
Align data	Select the cells, click the appropriate alignment button on the toolbar.
Change column width	Drag the column border to the desired width.
Format numbers as currency	Select the cells, click the Currency button on the toolbar.
Change the format of numbers	Select the cells, choose **F**ormat, **C**ells, click the Numbers tab, select the number type, select the number format, choose OK.
Add borders to cells	Select the cells, choose **F**ormat, **C**ells, click the Borders tab, select the border location, select the border style, choose OK.
Add patterns or shading to cells	Select the cells, choose **F**ormat, **C**ells, click the Patterns tab, choose the pattern or shading options, choose OK.
Automatically format a range	Select the cells, choose **F**ormat, **A**utoFormat, select the table format, choose OK.
Check spelling in a worksheet	Click the Spelling Checker button on the toolbar.
Copy formatting	Select the formatted cell. Click the Format Painter button. Select the cell(s) to format.

Applying Your Skills

Take a few minutes to practice the skills you have learned in this project by completing the following exercises.

Formatting the Travel Log

Practice using different formatting techniques to improve the appearance of a worksheet. Add the name of your business, make the column headings stand out, adjust coumn widths, add borders or patterns, and check the spelling in the worksheet.

To Format the Travel Log

1. Open the file Proj0303 and save it as **Travel 2**.
2. Add the name of your business to the top of the worksheet, and center it across the row.
3. Make the column headings stand out by changing the font, font size, and attributes.
4. Change the date formats. (*Hint:* Use the Format Painter button.)
5. Adjust column widths to fit all the data.
6. Change the date formats.
7. Format the Reimbursement total in cell B18 as currency.
8. Add borders or patterns to highlight the Reimbursement total, and to draw attention to the total mileage.
9. Check the spelling and add proper names to your personal dictionary, if you want.
10. Save the worksheet. If requested by your instructor, print two copies. Then close the file.

To Format the Ad Campaign Analysis

1. Open the file Proj0304 and save it as **Ad Budget 2**.
2. Add the name of your business to the worksheet.
3. Use the AutoFormat feature to apply an appropriate table format, if you want.
4. Check the spelling and add the date and time, if you want.
5. Save the worksheet. If requested by your instructor, print two copies. Then close it.

To Format the Paper Costs Budget

1. Open the file Proj0305 and save it as **Paper Costs 2**.
2. Add the name of your business to the worksheet.

Project 3: Improving the Appearance of a Worksheet

3. Use the AutoFormat feature to apply an appropriate table format.

4. Check the spelling and add the date and time, if you want.

5. Save the worksheet. If requested by your instructor, print two copies. Then close it.

Formatting Your Music Collection Worksheet

Use the Music Collection worksheet you created in Project 1 to practice formatting techniques. Apply the proper number format where needed, make the headings stand out, and change the text font to add interest. You can also add borders and shading to highlight important cells. Don't forget to check your spelling as well.

To Format Your Music Collection Worksheet

1. Open the file Proj0306 and save it as **Music Collection 2**.

2. Make formatting changes as suggested. Be creative, but also try to keep the formatting clean and simple so that the worksheet will look professional.

3. Check the spelling in the worksheet.

4. Save your changes to the worksheet. If requested by your instructor, print two copies. Then close it.

Checking Your Skills

True/False

For each of the following, check T or F to indicate whether the statement is true or false.

__T __F 1. You can quickly adjust the column width to fit the column contents by double-clicking the line between two columns.

__T __F 2. If the Font button on the Formatting toolbar displays no font name, you can still click the button and choose a font.

__T __F 3. When aligning text in a cell, you can align it both horizontally and vertically.

__T __F 4. You can add a border to one cell or to a group of cells but you cannot add shading to more than one cell at a time.

__T __F 5. You can add the name of the city you live in to the Spelling Checker dictionary so that it doesn't question you every time it comes across that name.

Checking Your Skills

Multiple Choice

Circle the letter of the correct answer for each of the following.

1. Which of the following is *not* an option in the Spelling dialog box?
   a. **I**gnore
   b. **C**hange
   c. **A**dd to Dictionary
   d. **A**lternatives

2. Which of the following is *not* a method of adjusting column width?
   a. **S**tyle, **C**olumn Width command
   b. Format, **C**olumn, Width command
   c. double-clicking the right column border on the worksheet frame
   d. dragging the column border on the worksheet frame

3. Which of the following *cannot* be formatted using the Formatting toolbar?
   a. fonts
   b. type size
   c. column width
   d. numerical formatting

4. Which of the following would the Spelling Checker *not* question?
   a. CApital
   b. Paycheck
   c. CBA
   d. Chekcing Account

5. If pound signs (######) fill a cell, it means that _____.
   a. the cell is not active
   b. the formula is impossible
   c. the column is not wide enough
   d. you must recalculate the formula

Completion

In the blank provided, write the correct answer for each of the following statements.

1. The mouse pointer changes to a _____ when you copy style formatting.

2. Add words to the Spelling Checker dictionary such as cities, _____, or technical terms.

3. When formatting a number to currency, you can use the _____ _____ tool to add decimal places.

4. If you want to enter a date, you can use hyphens between the month, day, and year, or use _____.

5. You can use the Orientation option in the Alignment tab of the Format Cells dialog box, to align text horizontally or _____.

Project 4

Calculating with Functions

Projecting Office Expenses

In this project, you learn how to
- Name Ranges
- Use Named Ranges
- Use Functions
- Build Formulas with Functions
- Use Conditional Statements

Why Would I Do This?

In Project 2, you learned to create formulas to calculate values in your worksheet, and you learned to use cell addresses to refer to specific cells. You also learned how to use simple functions to help speed up your work with formulas. In this project, you learn about range naming, another useful feature of Excel that can help you create formulas.

The **I**nsert, **N**ame command lets you assign an English name to a value or a formula in a single cell or a range of cells. You can then use the assigned name rather than the cell addresses when specifying cells that you want to use.

In this project, you learn how to project the costs of rent, paper, and other supplies for your office for the coming months by using range names and functions. You also learn how to use conditional statements to provide different answers depending on the results of your calculations.

Lesson 1: Naming Ranges

When you create a worksheet and plan to use a cell or range of cells many times, you may want to name the range. For example, you may want to name the range containing the total income so that you can easily use the income range in formulas. Rather than looking up the address of the range, you can simply name the range *income*, and use the range name in the formula in place of the range address. You can also use range names in other Excel commands and to move around the worksheet.

Range names can be up to 255 characters long, but you should keep them short so that you can easily remember the names and so that you have more room to enter the formula. Range names up to 15 characters long can be displayed in most scrolling list boxes. Range names can be typed in upper- or lowercase letters, but you cannot include spaces. Names must begin with a letter or underscore and can include any characters except spaces, math operators, or hyphens (-). You can use numbers in the name but you cannot start the name with a number. It is helpful not to use a combination of letters and numbers that look like a cell address (such as a34), because that can be confusing. Use names such as *expenses*, *income*, and *average*, that refer to the contents or use of the range.

Try naming ranges using the sample office expenses worksheet supplied for this project.

To Name Ranges

1. Open the file **Proj0401** and save it as **Office**.
2. Select cells B3 through C4.

   These are the first cells you want to name.

Lesson 1: Naming Ranges

3 **Open the Insert menu, move the mouse pointer to the Name command, and then choose Define from the nested menu that appears.**

The Define Name dialog box appears (see Figure 4.1).

Figure 4.1
Use the Define Name dialog box to name ranges.

Names in Workbook text box

Refers to text box

4 **Replace the default name, Paper_stationery, in the Names in Workbook text box, with paper96.**

This name describes the cells in the range, which includes all your paper expenses for 1996.

5 **Choose OK.**

The selected range is now named paper96. Notice that the range name now appears in the Names box in the Formula bar. Now name another range.

6 **Select cells F3 through G4 in the worksheet.**

This selects the next range you want to name.

7 **Open the Insert menu, move the mouse pointer to the Name command, and choose Define from the nested menu that appears.**

This opens the Define Name dialog box again. Notice that the paper96 range name now appears in the Names in Workbook list.

8 **In the Names in Workbook text box, type paper97, then click the Add button.**

The new range name appears in the Names in Workbook list. Now try naming a range without closing the Define Names dialog box.

9 **In the Refers to text box, drag the mouse pointer across the current range to highlight it.**

This selects the current range address. You are going to replace the current range address with the next range you want to name.

continues

To Name Ranges (continued)

> **If you have problems...**
>
> Make sure that you select all the text in the Define Names dialog box. If you don't select all the text, you will get an invalid range. Also, don't click any other control in the dialog box, or you won't be able to perform the next step.

🔟 Select cells B5 through C6 in the worksheet.

This is the range you want to name. If necessary, move the dialog box out of the way so that you can better see the worksheet. In the Define Name dialog box, the **R**efers to text box displays the new range address, as shown in Figure 4.2.

Figure 4.2
You can name additional ranges without closing the Define Name dialog box.

New range address

⓫ In the Names in Workbook text box, replace paper97 with supplies96, and then choose Add.

The supplies96 range includes all your supplies expenses for 1996. Now name one more range.

⓬ In the Refers to text box, highlight the existing range, and then select cells F5 through G6 in the worksheet.

⓭ Name this range supplies97, and then choose Add.

You have now named four ranges that you can use later to build formulas and move around the worksheet. All four are listed in the Define Name dialog box.

⓮ Choose OK to close the dialog box.

Click anywhere outside the selected cells to better see your worksheet. Save your work and keep the Office worksheet open to use in the next lesson.

Lesson 2: Using Named Ranges

You can use a named range in any formula to quickly and easily refer to a specific cell or range of cells. You can also use the Name box in the Formula bar to quickly move to and select a named range. Now practice using named ranges to move around the Office worksheet.

To Use Named Ranges

1 **In the Office worksheet, click the drop-down arrow to the right of the Name box in the Formula bar.**

This displays a list of the named ranges you created for this worksheet (see Figure 4.3).

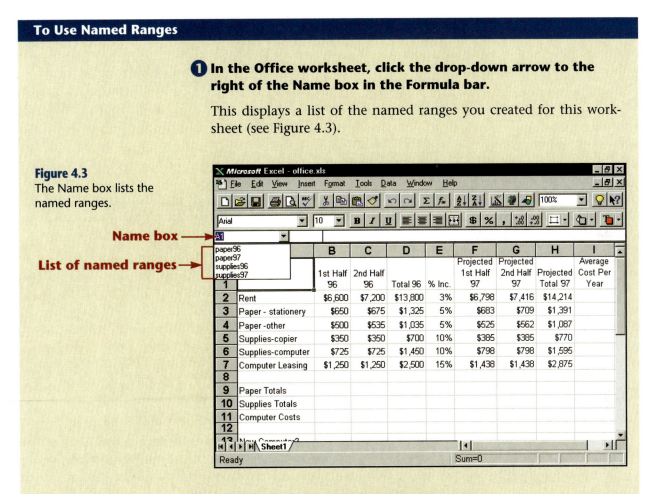

Figure 4.3
The Name box lists the named ranges.

2 **From the Name box list, select paper97.**

This selects the range paper97, as shown in Figure 4.4. You can now edit, copy, move, or otherwise modify the named range. This shortcut for moving to named ranges is especially useful when you create workbooks that contain multiple worksheets. Now try moving to another named range.

continues

To Use Named Ranges (continued)

Figure 4.4
Selecting the name of the range in the Name box list selects the entire range of cells.

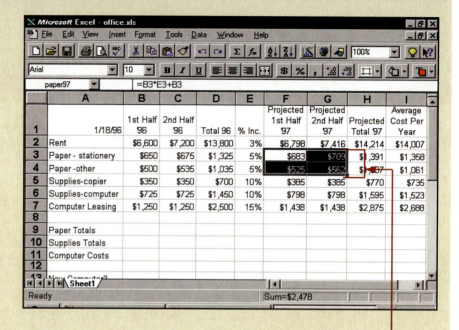

Selected range

❸ Click the Name box drop-down arrow, and select supplies96.

The supplies96 range is now selected in the worksheet. Notice that the name of the range appears in the Name box. Save your work and keep the Office worksheet open. You use range names and functions to continue creating the worksheet in the next lesson.

You can delete a named range by choosing **I**nsert, **N**ame, and then **D**efine from the submenu to open the Define Name dialog box. In the Define Name dialog box, select the name in the Names in **W**orkbook list and choose **D**elete. Choose OK to close the dialog box. If you have a cell with a formula that uses a named range, and you delete the definition of that named range, that cell will display #NAME?

In Excel, you can also name your worksheets and reference them in formulas. (As you learned in Project 1, each Excel file is called a workbook, and each workbook is made up of one or more worksheets.) At the bottom of each worksheet is a sheet tab, with the default sheet name on it. The first sheet is called Sheet1, the second sheet is called Sheet2, and so on. To view a different sheet, click the sheet tab. To change a sheet name, double-click the sheet tab, type the new name in the **N**ame text box of the Rename Sheet dialog box, and choose OK. To reference a worksheet, you type the worksheet name, followed by an exclamation point, followed by the cell address, range address, or range name. For example, if you have a workbook for a five-year forecast, with each year's data on a different worksheet, you can reference the different worksheets to create formulas to total, average, or in other ways work with the data from each worksheet.

Lesson 3: Using Functions

> **If you have problems...**
>
> If you use a range name in a formula before you assign the name, Excel returns the error message #NAME?. Name the range first, and then you can use it in a formula.
>
> If you receive an error message dialog box when using the named range in a formula, check for spaces, math operators, or numbers at the beginning of the name, or in the name of the range. If the name contains any of these, remove the symbol or number and try your formula again. To make changes, you must first respond to the dialog box, choose OK to make changes to your name, or choose **H**elp to get on-line help from Excel.

Lesson 3: Using Functions

As you learned in Project 2, functions are shortened formulas that perform specific operations on a group of values. Excel provides more than 200 functions that fit into 11 categories to help you with tasks such as determining loan payments and calculating interest on your savings.

In Project 2, you used the SUM function to total a column of numbers, so you already know that SUM is the function to automatically add entries in a range. The TODAY function is another common function used to include the date in a report or to use the date in calculations.

Table 4.1 describes other common functions used in Excel. Try using functions to build the Office worksheet now.

To Use Functions

1 **Select cell A1 in the Office worksheet.**

To enter a function, you can either type it directly in the cell or the Formula bar.

2 **Type =today() and click the Enter button (the green check mark) on the Formula bar.**

This is the TODAY function. Excel enters the system date in cell A1. You can change the format of the date if you want, as you learned in Project 3. Now enter a function to find the total amount you will spend on paper in 1996.

3 **Select cell D9.**

This is the cell where you want to enter the function.

4 **Click the Function Wizard button on the Standard toolbar.**

The Function Wizard Step 1 of 2 dialog box opens. It displays a list of functions grouped by category. The functions in the Most

continues

To Use Functions (continued)

Recently Used category are displayed in the Function **N**ame list box, as shown in Figure 4.5.

Figure 4.5
The Function Wizard dialog box displays the list of functions by category.

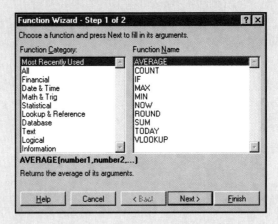

5 **In the Function Name list box, select SUM.**

SUM (number1, number2,...) appears in parentheses in cell D9 and in the Formula bar. The entire function appears selected, ready for you to click the Next button on the bottom of the dialog box to enter the *arguments*, or range of cells, that you want to total.

6 **Click the Next button in the Function Wizard dialog box.**

The Function Wizard Step 2 of 2 dialog box appears, as shown in Figure 4.6.

Figure 4.6
The second Function Wizard dialog box.

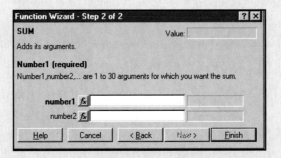

7 **In the number1 text box, type paper96, and then choose Finish.**

This enters the range paper96 into the formula as the *argument*. The amount spent for paper in 1996 now appears in cell D9 (see Figure 4.7).

Figure 4.7
Create a formula using the named range.

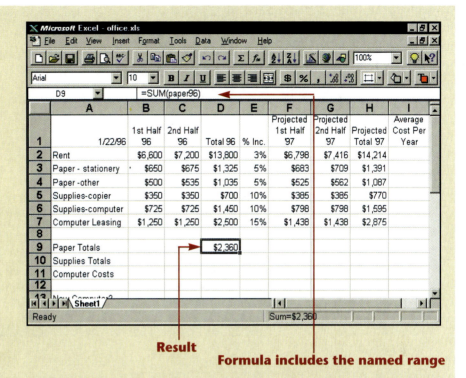

Result **Formula includes the named range**

If you have problems...

If you enter a function with a mistake in it, #NAME? appears in the cell, or Excel refuses to enter the formula in the cell and goes into edit mode, where you can correct the mistake. First, make sure that you used an existing named range, and then check for typos in the range name.

Study the formula and check the range name for exclamation points, commas, periods, semicolons, question marks, plus or minus signs, asterisks, slashes, ampersands, less than or greater than signs, at signs, pound signs, or numbers at the beginning of the name. The error message #NAME? will appear if your range name contains any of these symbols. Remove the offending symbol or number and try again.

Now enter functions to total the rest of your paper and supplies expenses for 1996 and 1997.

 8 In cell D10, type =sum(supplies96), and then press Enter.

The sum showing the total spent for supplies in 1996 appears in the cell. You can also click the Enter button.

 9 Select cell H9, then click the AutoSum button on the Standard toolbar.

The SUM function, with the incorrect range as the argument, appears in cell H9.

continues

Project 4 Calculating with Functions

To Use Functions (continued)

 10 **From the Name box drop-down list, select paper97, then click the Enter button on the Formula bar.**

This replaces the incorrect range in the formula with the correct range—paper97, and enters the formula. The projected total paper expenses for 1997 appears in cell H9. You can either type the function, use the Function Wizard and Name box list, or use the SUM button and the Name box list (or you can use a combination of these methods).

11 **In cell H10, enter =sum(supplies97), and then press ↵Enter.**

The projected total expense for supplies in 1997 appears. Your worksheet should now look similar to the one shown in Figure 4.8. Save your work and keep the Office worksheet open for the next lesson, where you create more complex formulas with functions.

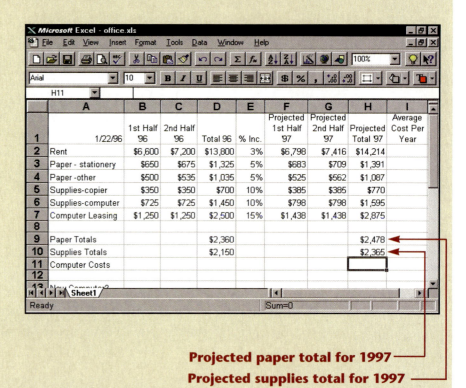

Figure 4.8
Use functions to project the costs of paper and supplies for 1997.

Projected paper total for 1997
Projected supplies total for 1997

If you have problems...

If you think a function that uses a range is not returning the correct answer, make sure that the range is entered correctly. Ensure that all cells that you need are included and that no extra cells containing data are included.

Lesson 3: Using Functions

Jargon Watch

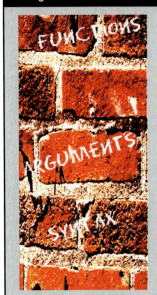

Several differences exist between regular formulas and **functions**. One difference is that you can customize regular formulas more to your liking. You use functions as shortcuts to tell Excel how to calculate values.

As demonstrated in Project 2, entering the function =SUM(B2:B9) is quicker and easier than entering the formula =B2+B3+B4+B5+B6+B7+B8+B9. In a regular formula, you must specify every operation to be performed. That's why so many plus signs are in the preceding formula. In a function, however, the operations are programmed in, so you need only supply the necessary information in the form of **arguments**. In the function =SUM(B2:B9), (B2:B9) is the argument.

When you add arguments to a function, you must use the proper **syntax**. Syntax is simply the exact and correct way to type commands and functions. In general, computer programs are inflexible about even one wrong keystroke, such as a missing comma.

If your formula returns the error message #NAME?, use the Excel Help feature to find out more about the syntax for the specific function you are trying to use.

Instead of typing a range into a function, you can use the mouse to select the range. For example, you can type **=SUM(** and then drag the mouse to select the range. Excel enters the range in the Formula bar as you drag. End the function by pressing ↵Enter to calculate the formula.

An easy way to enter the name of a range in a function or formula is to type = and then the **function name**, an **open parenthesis**, and then press F3. The Paste Name dialog box appears with a list of named ranges. Choose the name of the range from the Paste **N**ame list box. Choose OK to close the dialog box, and then press ↵Enter.

Also, don't forget that you can quickly check the result of a calculation without actually entering the formula by using the AutoCalculate button on the status bar.

Table 4.1 Common Functions		
Function	Category	Description
AVERAGE	Statistical	Displays the average of a list of values.
CELL	Information	Returns information about a cell or its contents.
DATE	Date & Time	Lists the date according to the computer's clock.
ERROR.TYPE	Information	Displays a number corresponding to one of Excel's error values. Used to debug macros and worksheets.
EVEN	Math & Trig	Rounds a value up to the nearest even integer.
MAX	Statistical	Finds the largest value in a list of numbers.
MIN	Statistical	Finds the smallest value in a list of numbers.

continues

Project 4 Calculating with Functions

Table 4.1 Continued		
Function	Category	Description
NOW	Date & Time	Calculates the current date and time on the computer's clock.
ODD	Math & Trig	Rounds a value up to the nearest odd integer.
PMT	Financial	Calculates the periodic payment amount needed to pay off a loan.
PRODUCT	Math & Trig	Calculates the product of a list of values by multiplying each value in turn.
ROUND	Math & Trig	Rounds a value to a specific number of decimal places.
SUM	Math & Trig	Adds a list of values.
TIME	Date & Time	Lists the time according to the computer's clock.
TODAY	Date & Time	Calculates the serial number for the current date and is used for date and time calculations.

Lesson 4: Building Formulas with Functions

Nest
Place one function within another function.

Functions are easy to use in building complex formulas. For example, you can add two SUM functions together, as you do in this lesson using the Office worksheet. You can also *nest* functions by using functions as arguments for other functions.

This lesson shows you how to create complex formulas by combining and nesting functions.

To Build Formulas with Functions

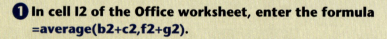

❶ **In cell I2 of the Office worksheet, enter the formula =average(b2+c2,f2+g2).**

This enters the formula and calculates the average cost of rent per year. Don't forget to click the Enter button on the Formula bar.

Note that you can get the same result from the simple formula =average(d2,h2). In general, it's best to use the simplest formula possible in your worksheets. You have been asked to build more complex formulas in this lesson to learn how functions can be used together.

Lesson 4: Building Formulas with Functions

> **If you have problems...**
>
> If the average doesn't appear to be correct, make sure that the ranges you used don't include any extra cells with values or labels. When writing an AVERAGE formula, be sure to use only the specific cells of the contents you want to average.

❷ Select cell I2 again, click the right mouse button to open the shortcut menu, and then choose Copy.

This copies the formula in cell I2 to the Windows Clipboard.

❸ Select cells I3 through I7, open the shortcut menu and choose Paste.

This copies the formula to cells I3 through I7, where the results are displayed, as shown in Figure 4.9 (because no decimal places are displayed, Excel rounds the totals to the nearest whole number; however, the actual value is used in all calculations). The formulas in the cells are relative. In Project 2, you learned that *relative* means the formula relates to its current address, no matter where it was first entered. In this example, the formula is always relative to the numbers in the cells to the left of the formula's current cell address.

Figure 4.9
The function averages the values relative to its current cell address.

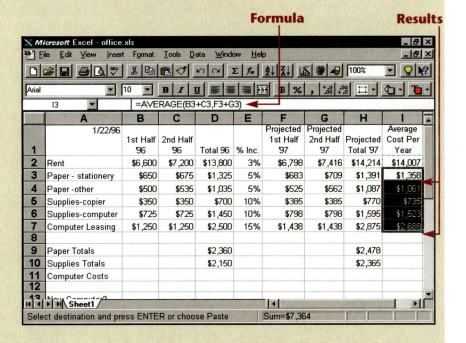

 ❹ In cell D11, enter the formula =sum(b6:c6)+sum(b7:c7).

This calculates the total computer costs for 1996, by adding together the total costs of computer supplies and the total costs of

continues

To Build Formulas with Functions (continued)

computer leasing. You have built the formula by combining two functions with the + sign.

(Once again, you are using more complex formulas than are necessary. You can get the same result with the simple formula =D6+D7, which adds the total computer supplies and computer leasing expenses for the year.)

Now enter a formula to calculate the total computer costs for 1997.

5 In cell H11, use the mouse to select the range arguments to enter the formula =sum(f6:g6)+sum(f7:g7).

Again, you combine two SUM functions to create the formula. The projected total computer costs for 1997 appear in cell H11, as shown in Figure 4.10.

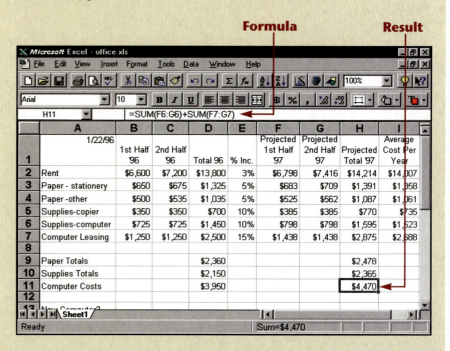

Figure 4.10
You can combine functions to create more complex functions.

Now create a complex formula to calculate the average total computer costs per year. Use your choice of either the mouse or keyboard to enter the formula.

6 In cell I11, enter the formula =average(sum(b6:c7),sum(f6:g7)).

By combining several functions, you have created a formula that calculates the average total computer costs per year, as shown in Figure 4.11. Again, note that you can also achieve the same result with the simpler formula AVERAGE(D11,H11), which adds the total costs for 1996 and 1997, and then finds the average of the two. Note also that D11 equals SUM(D6:D7), and that H11 equals

Lesson 4: Building Formulas with Functions

SUM(H6:H7). In creating the more complex formula, you have simply replaced the SUM functions for cells D11 and H11.

Figure 4.11
You can nest formulas to perform several calculations at once.

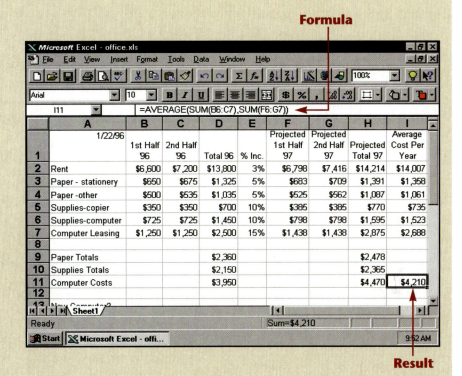

You have now created formulas to calculate all the information you need to track your office expenses. Save your work and keep the Office worksheet open for the next lesson, where you use a function to tell you whether you would save money by purchasing a personal computer.

If you have problems...

A common mistake in complex functions involves parentheses. Be sure that for every open parenthesis there is a corresponding closed parenthesis. All parentheses must be placed in the correct location to avoid a syntax error.

Another fairly common mistake is substituting a + sign for the colon in a SUM formula. SUM(D10:I10) is much different than SUM(D10+I10); in the latter formula, only the first and last cells are added, whereas in the first formula, all cells from D10 to I10 including D10 and I10 are added.

If Excel responds with the error message #NAME?, don't worry. Simply check your formula carefully to make sure that all parentheses are present and all addresses are correct. If you still can't find the problem, check the values and formulas in the referenced cells for typos. One typographical error can affect formulas in many parts of the worksheet if the formulas reference the cell containing the error.

Project 4 Calculating with Functions

A colon between the cell address in a range argument is simply the standard method that Excel uses to show the range.

When you paste a formula from one cell into another, each cell reference in the original formula is converted to a relative reference. For example, if the formula in cell C5 references B3, that reference is converted to the cell one column to the left and two rows up when the formula is copied to the clipboard. Pasting that formula into cell F9 translates the relative reference back into an absolute reference—in this case E7, which is one column to the left and two rows up from the destination.

Lesson 5: Using Conditional Statements

Your Office worksheet now contains all the information and formulas that you need to track the cost of running an office over two years. Now look at how you can have the worksheet calculate whether you should purchase computer equipment instead of continuing to lease it.

Using conditional statements, you can implement different actions depending on whether a condition is true or false. The simplest conditional function in Excel is IF. You can use this function to get one answer if the condition is true and another if it is false.

Try using the IF function to see whether your computer costs are sufficiently high to warrant purchasing a personal computer.

To Use Conditional Statements

❶ Select cell B13 of the Office worksheet.

❷ Click the Function Wizard button.

This opens the Function Wizard Step 1 of 2 dialog box.

❸ Choose Logical in the Function Category list, and then choose IF in the Function Name list.

Excel displays `=IF(logical_test,value_if_true,value_if_false)` in cell B13 and in the Formula bar (see Figure 4.12).

Lesson 5: Using Conditional Statements

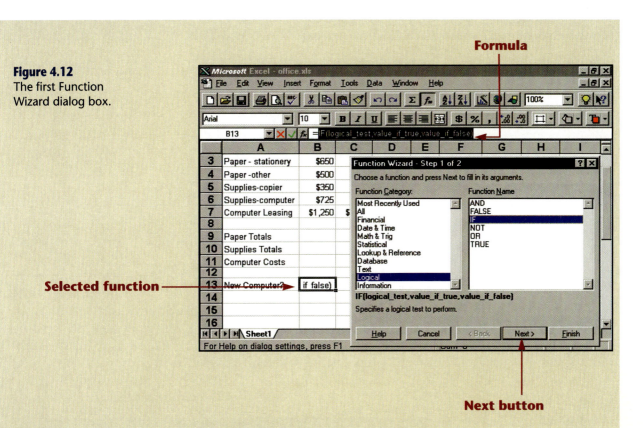

Figure 4.12
The first Function Wizard dialog box.

The condition is the if part of the statement. For this example, *if* your total average computer costs for a year are more than $4,000, *then* it makes sense to purchase a computer.

4 **Choose Next to build the argument for the IF function.**

The Function Wizard Step 2 of 2 dialog box appears (see Figure 4.13).

5 **In the logical_test text box, type I11>4000, and press Tab.**

This replaces the condition with a mathematical way of saying the if statement above, and moves you to the next text box. I11 refers to the cell where the average total computer costs are calculated, the > sign is the mathematical operator that means greater than, and 4000 is the value you want to use for comparison.

6 **In the value_if_true text box, type YES!, including the exclamation mark, and press Tab.**

The value_if_true box is the second argument of the function that tells Excel what you want to have in the cell if the condition is true. In other words, if the total average cost per year is greater than $4,000, Excel will enter YES! in the current cell.

7 **In the value_if_false box, type NO.**

The value_if_false box is the final argument. It tells Excel what to enter in the current cell if the condition is false—meaning if the value in cell I11 is less than $4,000. The Function Wizard dialog box should now look like the one in Figure 4.13.

continues

To Use Conditional Statements (continued)

Figure 4.13
The second Function Wizard dialog box for creating a conditional formula.

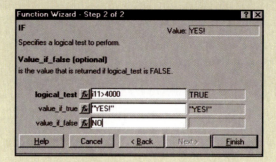

8 Choose Finish.

Excel performs the calculation, and the word YES! should now appear in cell B13, as shown in Figure 4.14. When you use the IF function, Excel tells you that you should purchase the computer based on the information currently in the worksheet. If the projected expenses were to decrease so that the average total was less than $4,000, Excel would return *NO* as the response.

Figure 4.14
The result of the conditional statement is "Yes!".

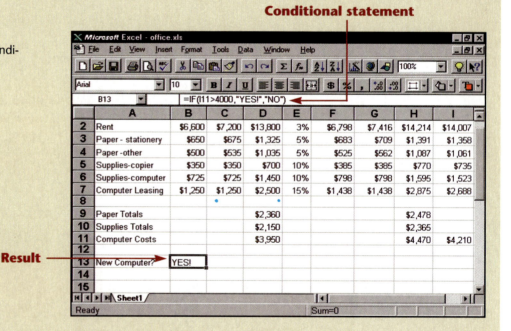

Save your work. If requested by your instructor, print two copies. Then close the worksheet. If you have completed your session on the computer, exit Excel for Windows and Windows 95 before turning off the computer. Otherwise, continue with the "Applying Your Skills" section at the end of this project.

Applying Your Skills

Jargon Watch

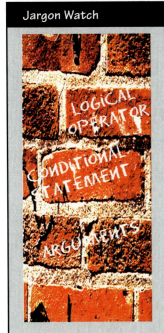

Conditional statements use many mathematical terms that can be confusing. In most cases, however, a **conditional statement** takes the form of a simple if/then sentence—if this happens, then that happens.

Conditional statements or arguments, such as the one in this lesson, typically use a **logical operator**. Logical operators include the following:

Operator	Meaning
=	Equals
<	Less than
>	Greater than
>=	Greater than or equal to
<=	Less than or equal to

Think of these operators simply as replacements for the words in the Meaning column above.

Project Summary

To	Do This
Name a Range	Select the range, choose **I**nsert, **N**ame, **D**efine, type a name in the Names in **W**orkbook text box, and choose OK.
Select a Named Range	Click the drop-down arrow in the Name box in the Formula bar, and choose the range name.
Start the Function Wizard	Click the Function Wizard button on the Standard toolbar.
Perform what-if analysis on data	Use the Logical IF function.

Applying Your Skills

Take a few minutes to practice the skills you have learned in this project by completing the following exercises.

Checking Sales Figures

As the owner and business manager of Sound Byte Music, you need to evaluate the performance of the merchandise you stock in your store. You want to know if you are buying the right mix of music to sell to your customers.

To find out if you are buying the right music, use the sample sales figures provided in Proj0402 to calculate total sales for the first quarter in each category of music. Devise a formula using conditional statements that will alert you if sales of any category fall below a certain level. If necessary, use the Excel Help feature to find out more about the function you use.

To Check Sales Figures

1. Start Windows and Excel.
2. Open the file Proj0402 and save it as **Sales Figures**.
3. In the Total column, create a formula to calculate the total sales for January, February, and March for each type of music. Have the formula round the totals to 0 decimal places. *Hint:* Use more than one function.
4. In the Check column, use functions to return a message that either warns of sales below a minimum level of $500, or reports that sales are OK. Include this check for each category of music you sell.
5. Save your work. If requested by your instructor, print two copies of the completed worksheet. Then close it.

Calculating Future Salary Requirements

You can use functions and formulas to determine whether your business can support increasing salaries. Use the data provided to calculate the amount of money spent on current salaries, and to forecast projected salaries.

To Calculate Future Salary Requirements

1. Open the file Proj0403 and save it as **Salaries**.
2. Calculate the projected salaries.
3. Calculate the average current salary, and the average projected salary.
4. Calculate the total amount of all current salaries and all projected salaries.
5. Use a conditional statement to determine whether you will be able to increase salaries as proposed. To make the decision, assume that if the average projected salary is less than $22,500, you can afford increases.
6. Change the proposed increase percentages to see how the conditional statement is affected.
7. Save your work. If requested by your instructor, print two copies before closing the document.

Creating a Worksheet to Calculate Grade Point Average

Create a worksheet that calculates your grade point average for each class you have this semester as well as your total grade point average. Use a conditional statement that will tell you whether you will make the Dean's List with your current grades.

To Create the Grade Point Average Worksheet

1. Start Windows and Excel.
2. Open the file Proj0404 and save it as **Grades**.
3. In the Point Value column, convert each grade to points using the following system: A = 4 points; B = 3 points; C = 2 points; D = 1 point; and F = 0.
4. To find your overall grade point average, create a formula to average your grades for each class.
5. Create a conditional statement that tells you whether you can expect to make the Dean's List. For this case study, the Dean's List includes all students with a 3.0 grade point average or higher.
6. Save the worksheet. If requested by your instructor, print two copies. Then close it.

Calculating Utility Expenses

Create a worksheet that calculates your average utility expenses to determine whether or not you can afford cable television.

To Calculate Utility Expenses

1. Open the file Proj0405 and save it as **Utility Expenses**.
2. Calculate the average cost per month of each utility, and the total average monthly cost of all utilities.
3. Use a conditional statement to determine whether or not you can afford cable T.V. For this example, your utility costs must be $600 or less for you to be able to afford cable.
4. Save the worksheet. If requested by your instructor, print two copies before closing it.

Checking Your Skills

True/False

For each of the following, check *T* or *F* to indicate whether the statement is true or false.

__T __F **1.** You can name a range but not an individual cell.

__T __F **2.** Range names can consist of up to 255 characters.

__T __F **3.** If Excel displays the error message #NAME? when using a named range in a formula, check to make sure you have the = sign in the name.

__T __F **4.** An IF statement includes a condition and two arguments.

__T __F **5.** Using a Date and Time function automatically formats the cell to date or time.

Multiple Choice

Circle the letter of the correct answer for each of the following.

1. _____ is a collection of cells that you can use in a formula.
    a. B2...B2
    b. B2:G2
    c. B2:G2,B6
    d. B4+C4,C6

2. Which of the following is a valid formula?
    a. =AVERAGE(B2;C2;D4;G4)
    b. =SUM(B2:B8)-AVG(D2:D4)
    c. =SUM(AVG(C3;C4),(AVG F6:F9))
    d. =SUM(SUM(C3:C9,SUM(D3:D9))

3. Which of the following is a valid range name?
    a. tuitionandfees96
    b. tuition_1996
    c. tuition fees
    d. tuition&fees

4. When using the IF conditional statement, you can _____.
    a. set a condition and get one answer if the condition is true and a second answer if the condition is false
    b. set one condition and one argument to analyze a formula
    c. enter a condition that performs a calculation on a formula
    d. list between two and six arguments that apply to the IF condition

5. Which of the following could cause the error message #NAME? to be returned as a result?
    a. using too many functions
    b. using the wrong named ranges
    c. using too many parentheses
    d. using the wrong symbols for operators

Completion

In the blank provided, write the correct answer for each of the following statements.

1. The _____ in the Formula bar lists named ranges.

2. When you use a named range in a formula before you assign the name, Excel returns a(n) _____ in the cell.

Checking Your Skills

3. You can combine or _____ functions within a formula so that you can perform complex calculations at one time.

4. The _____ is always placed in parentheses to indicate which data the function will use to perform its calculation.

5. The _____ _____ is on the Standard toolbar and takes you through the steps to building functions.

Project 5

Using Charts and Maps

Charting Income

In this project, you learn how to
- Create a Chart
- Format Text in a Chart
- Change the Chart Type
- Enhance a Chart
- Print a Chart
- Create a Map

Why Would I Do This?

After you create a worksheet, you may want to show the information to someone else. You can simply print the worksheet if you need only numerical detail, or you can transform the information in the worksheet into a chart. With Excel for Windows 95, you can also chart geographic information with maps. Charts and maps are great for visually representing relationships between numerical values while improving the appearance of a presentation at the same time.

This project shows you how to use sample data to create and enhance various types of charts. You also learn how to add a map to a worksheet.

Lesson 1: Creating a Chart

Embedded chart
A graphical representation of worksheet data created within the worksheet rather than as a separate document.

In Excel for Windows, you can create an embedded chart directly in the worksheet. An *embedded chart* is a graphic object—a picture of the data—that appears in the worksheet along with your worksheet data. You can also add a chart of the data to a separate worksheet.

You select the data you want to use in the chart and then draw a box or frame to hold the chart. Excel automatically creates the chart from the selected data, and you can then change or enhance the chart. Now try creating a chart to help you analyze your monthly office expenses.

To Create a Chart

❶ Open the file Proj0501 and save it as Expenses.

This is the workbook file you use in this project.

❷ Select cells A2 through G7.

This is the data you will use to create the chart. You can create a chart using any of the information in the worksheet. The range you selected here lets you see how your expense costs change over the course of six months.

 ❸ Click the ChartWizard button on the Standard toolbar.

The mouse pointer becomes a charting pointer, which you use to select the area in the worksheet where you want to display the chart.

❹ Click cell A9 and drag the pointer to cell H29, then release the mouse button.

This selects the range of cells in which Excel will place your finished chart. As you drag, notice the rectangular area defined on the worksheet. When you release the mouse button, Excel displays the ChartWizard Step 1 of 5 dialog box, as shown in Figure 5.1. The range of cells you want your chart to illustrate (A2:G7) is displayed in the **R**ange text box.

Lesson 1: Creating a Chart E-113

Figure 5.1
The ChartWizard Step 1 of 5 dialog box.

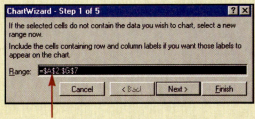

Selected range for chart information

❺ Click the Next button.

The ChartWizard Step 2 of 5 dialog box appears. For this example, the default chart type, **C**olumn, is satisfactory. Otherwise, you could select a different chart type (see Figure 5.2).

Default chart type

Figure 5.2
The ChartWizard Step 2 of 5 dialog box.

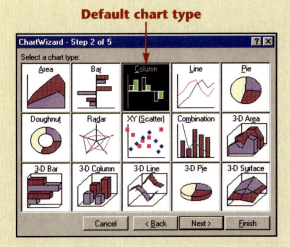

❻ Click the Next button.

The ChartWizard Step 3 of 5 dialog box appears, which lets you select the format for the chart type you have chosen. In this case, you use the default format for the Column chart.

❼ Click the Next button.

The default format is accepted and the ChartWizard Step 4 of 5 dialog box appears, as shown in Figure 5.3. A sample of the chart you are creating is displayed in the dialog box. If necessary, you can change the way the *data series* is displayed from rows to columns, but for this example, the default settings are fine.

continues

To Create a Chart (continued)

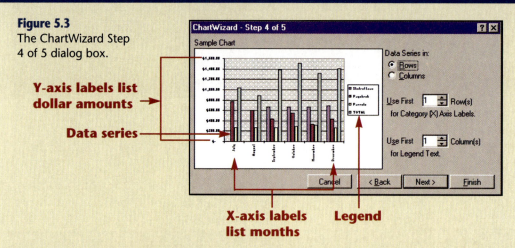

Figure 5.3
The ChartWizard Step 4 of 5 dialog box.

Y-axis labels list dollar amounts

Data series

X-axis labels list months

Legend

8 **Click the Next button.**

The defaults are accepted and the ChartWizard Step 5 of 5 dialog box appears (see Figure 5.4). Here, you can choose to hide the *legend*, add a chart *title*, and label the *axes*. You want the legend, so do not change that option.

9 **Click in the Chart Title text box, type Office Expenses and then press Tab.**

Excel adds the title to the chart and moves the insertion point to the Axis Titles, Category (**X**) text box.

10 **Type Months in the Axis Titles, Category (X) text box, press Tab, then type Dollars in the Value (Y) text box.**

Excel labels the axes on the chart. The ChartWizard Step 5 of 5 dialog box should now look like the one shown in Figure 5.4.

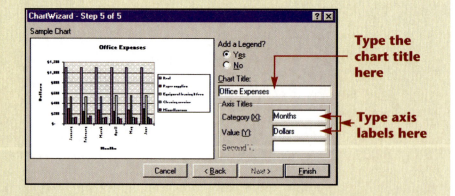

Figure 5.4
The ChartWizard Step 5 of 5 dialog box.

Type the chart title here

Type axis labels here

11 **Click the Finish button.**

Excel creates the chart in the range you selected (A9:H29) and displays the Chart toolbar, which you can use to edit the chart, as shown in Figure 5.5. You may have to scroll down in the worksheet to see the entire chart. Save your work and keep the Expenses worksheet open to use in the next lesson.

Lesson 1: Creating a Chart   E-115

Figure 5.5
Excel creates the chart in the range of cells you specified earlier.

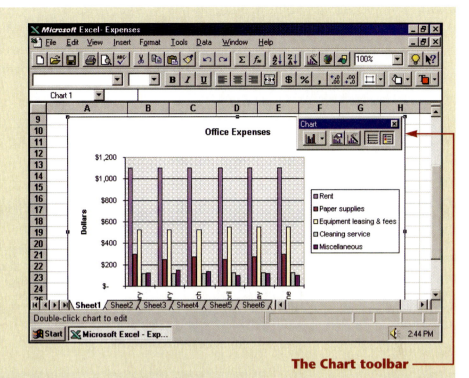

The Chart toolbar

Jargon Watch

Charts and maps are considered to be **objects** in Excel. An object is an item that has its own frame or box and can be selected, moved, copied, sized, and formatted independently of the worksheet cells behind it. Other objects include text blocks and clip art.

Charts consist of a number of elements, most of which you can modify or delete. A chart's **title**, for example, is simply the chart's name.

Charts can also include other text such as a **legend**, **notes**, and **data labels**. A legend tells what each color or symbol in the chart's data series represents. The **data series** is a range of values in a worksheet, such as the expense information you used to create the chart in Lesson 1. Notes are brief descriptions or explanations of the data in the chart. Data labels are names such as "Months" or "Dollars" that appear along the vertical and horizontal **axes** to describe the data in the chart.

The axes provide the scale used to measure the data in the chart. The **Y-axis** is the vertical line of the chart and the **X-axis** is the horizontal line.

Project 5 Using Charts and Maps

Lesson 2: Formatting Text in a Chart

After you create a chart, you can format text to enhance the chart's title, or you can change the emphasis of the chart's details. You can change text in a chart simply by clicking the text you want to modify and then making the change.

In Excel, you change the format of the text in charts using the same methods you use to format text in worksheet cells. Now try formatting text in the chart you created in Lesson 1.

To Format Text in a Chart

1 In the Expenses worksheet, scroll down until you can see as much of the chart as possible. When the chart is in full view, double-click the chart in the worksheet window.

The chart appears in its own document window, and the menu bar changes slightly as the Chart menu bar replaces the standard Excel menu bar (see Figure 5.6).

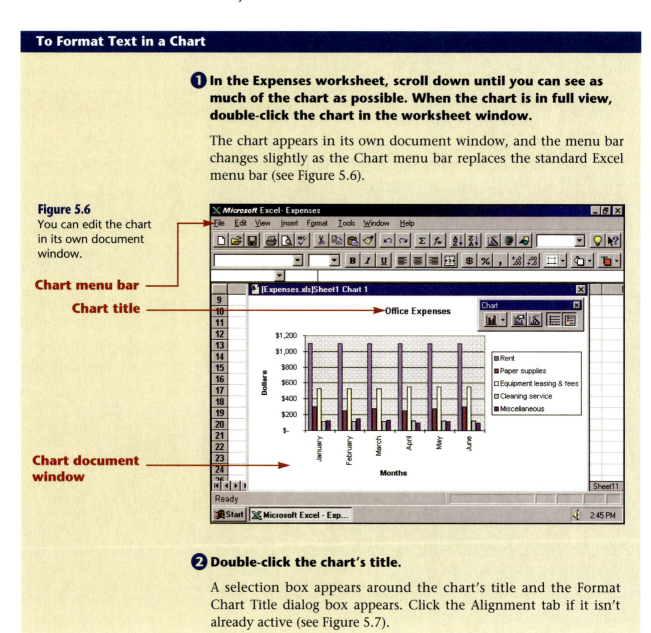

Figure 5.6
You can edit the chart in its own document window.

Chart menu bar
Chart title
Chart document window

2 Double-click the chart's title.

A selection box appears around the chart's title and the Format Chart Title dialog box appears. Click the Alignment tab if it isn't already active (see Figure 5.7).

Lesson 2: Formatting Text in a Chart

Figure 5.7
The Format Chart Title dialog box.

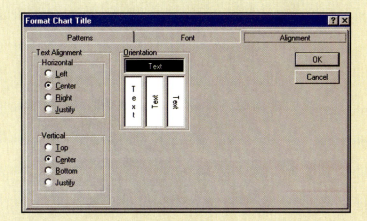

3 **Click the Font tab in the Chart Title dialog box.**

This displays the Font options that you can use to change the appearance of text in a chart.

4 **In the Font list, select Times New Roman.**

This changes the font from Arial to Times New Roman.

5 **In the Size list box, select 20, and then choose OK.**

This increases the size of the chart's title from 10 points to 20 points and closes the dialog box. Your chart should now resemble the one shown in Figure 5.8.

Figure 5.8
The chart title now appears in 20-point Times New Roman.

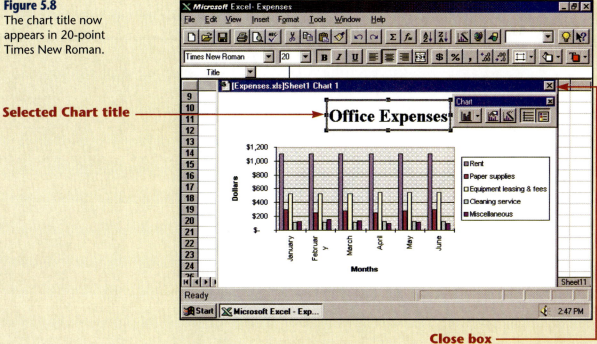

continues

Project 5   Using Charts and Maps

> **To Format Text in a Chart   (continued)**
>
> ❻ **Click the chart window's Close box.**
>
> This closes the chart window and returns you to your worksheet window with the embedded chart displayed. Save your work and keep the Expenses worksheet open. In Lesson 3, you learn how to change to other chart types.

Lesson 3: Changing the Chart Type

After you create a chart, you may decide you don't like the type of chart you have selected. Excel has a wide variety of chart types that you can choose from, to display information in a way that best conveys its meaning.

Certain chart types are best for certain situations. It's important to select a chart type that can help you display the information in the most dramatic, appropriate, and meaningful manner possible. For example, you can usually spot trends more easily with a line chart, while a pie chart is best for showing parts of a whole.

Now try changing the Expenses chart to a different type of chart.

> **To Change the Chart Type**
>
> ❶ **In the Expenses worksheet, click anywhere on the chart.**
>
> This selects the chart. Eight selection handles appear on the chart box frame to show that the chart is selected (see Figure 5.9). When you select the chart, the Chart toolbar automatically appears, so that the tools associated with charting are available for your use.
>
> ❷ **Click the drop-down arrow next to the Chart Type button on the Chart toolbar.**
>
> The various chart types are displayed in a two-column drop-down list (see Figure 5.10). If you can't see the Chart toolbar on your screen, choose **V**iew, **T**oolbars, and then click the Chart check box.

Lesson 3: Changing the Chart Type E-119

Figure 5.9
The selected chart has a border and selection handles.

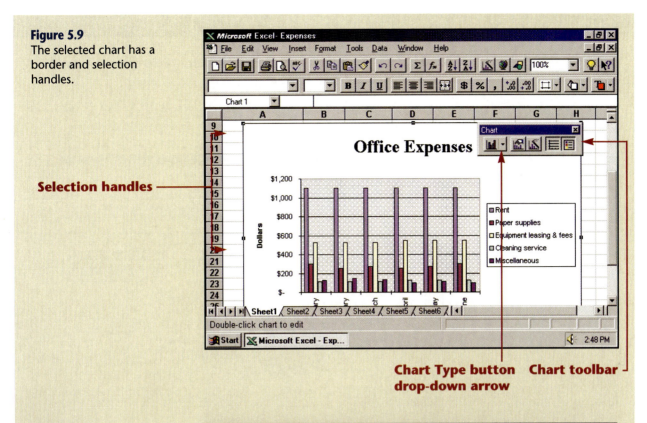

Figure 5.10
Select a chart type from the drop-down list.

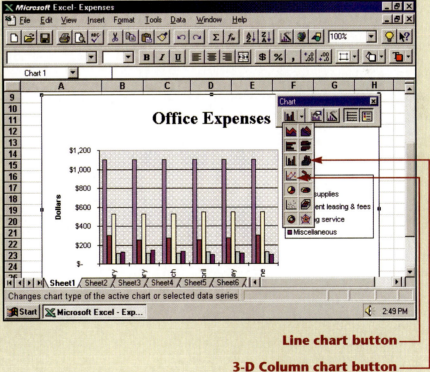

continues

To Change the Chart Type (continued)

❸ Click the 3-D Column chart button (the third button down in the right-hand column).

Excel changes the chart type to the 3-D vertical bar format, as shown in Figure 5.11.

Figure 5.11
The Expenses data appears as a 3-D column chart.

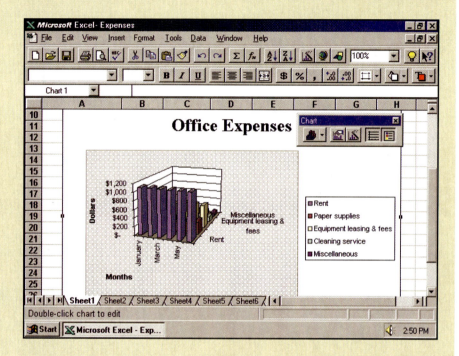

The 3-D column chart does not provide a very good representation of your data. If you want to examine the trends, over time, of the source of your income, there may be better chart types to use. Consult Table 5.1 to learn more about the different chart types available, and how they represent your data. Now select another type of chart that can more clearly illustrate the trend.

❹ From the Chart Type drop-down list, click the Line Chart button (the fourth button down in the left-hand column).

The chart type changes to a line chart (see Figure 5.12).

Lesson 3: Changing the Chart Type

Figure 5.12
In a line chart, you can easily examine trends over time.

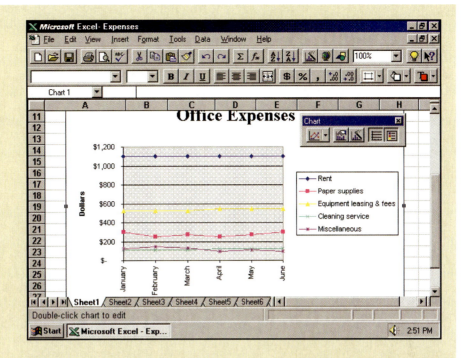

Table 5.1 describes the various chart types available in Excel. Save your work and keep the Expenses worksheet open. In Lesson 4, you learn how to enhance your chart's appearance.

If you have problems...

If you aren't sure which chart type to select for a specific job, select one chart type and study the results. Check to see whether the data is accurately represented and conveys the appropriate meaning. Try various chart types until you find the one that best suits your needs.

Table 5.1 Common Chart Types

Chart Type	Description
Area	A line chart that shows the area below the line filled with a color or pattern. Use an area chart to compare several sets of data.
Bar or Column	Represents data by the height of the vertical columns or length of the horizontal bars. Use a bar chart to compare one item to another or to compare different items over a period of time.
Line	Consists of a series of data at various points along the axis. The points are connected by a line. Use a line chart to indicate a trend over a period of time.

continues

Project 5 Using Charts and Maps

Table 5.1 Continued	
Chart Type	Description
Pie	A circular chart in which each piece (wedge) shows a data segment and its relationship to the whole. Use a pie chart to sort data and compare parts of the whole.
Doughnut	A circular, ring-shaped chart that compares the sizes of pieces in a whole. Similar to a pie chart.
Radar	A line or area chart enclosed around a central point. Use a radar chart to show the uniformity of data.
XY (Scatter)	A chart in which data points are placed along a numeric X-axis, similar to a line chart. Use an XY chart to compare large sets of data.
Combination	Combines parts from a line, bar, or area chart so that you can plot data in two forms on the same chart. Use a combination chart to show a correlation between two data series.
3-D (Area, Bar, Line, Pie)	Represents data in the same way as its two-dimensional counterpart. Besides displaying height and width, however, a 3-D chart adds depth to the appearance of the chart.

Lesson 4: Enhancing a Chart

After you have decided which type of chart best conveys the information in your worksheet, you can enhance the chart's appearance in several ways. The most common enhancements include changing chart colors, adding a grid, and formatting the chart labels.

The easiest way to change any part of a chart is to move the mouse pointer over the part you want to change, click the right mouse button, and then choose a command from the shortcut menu.

Now try using this easy method to enhance the Expenses chart.

To Enhance a Chart

1 In the Expenses worksheet, right-click the chart, then choose Edit Object from the shortcut menu.

The chart is displayed in a document window for you to edit.

2 Right-click one of the points of the line representing Rent in the chart.

A shortcut menu appears and the Rent line is selected, as shown in Figure 5.13.

Lesson 4: Enhancing a Chart   E–123

Figure 5.13
Each element of a chart has its own shortcut menu for editing.

Rent line

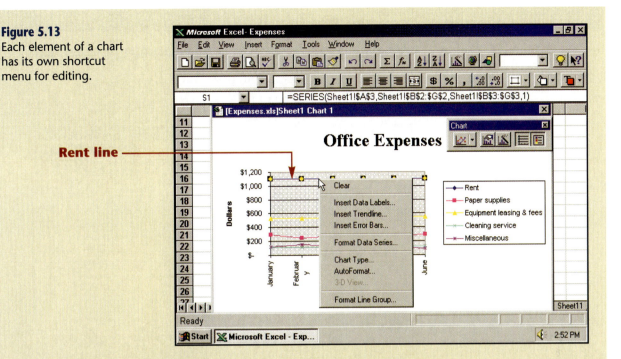

❸ Choose Chart Type from the shortcut menu.

The Chart Type dialog box appears (see Figure 5.14).

Figure 5.14
The Chart Type dialog box.

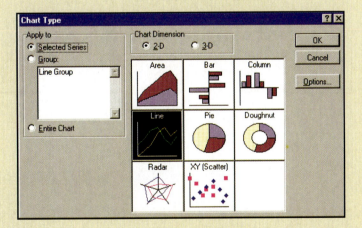

❹ Click the Area chart type, and then choose OK.

The chart is now a combination area and line chart, as shown in Figure 5.15. Rent, the element you selected to edit, is represented by the large blue area, while the rest of the chart remains unchanged. Now change the color of the total area.

continues

To Enhance a Chart (continued)

Figure 5.15
A combination area and line chart.

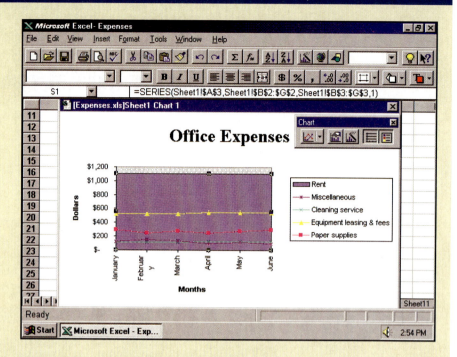

⑤ **Right-click the Rent area, and choose Format Data Series from the shortcut menu.**

The Format Data Series dialog box opens with the Patterns tab selected. In the Area section of the dialog box, a palette of colors is displayed. The current color for the Rent area is shown in the Sample box in the lower right corner.

⑥ **Select gray, the second color down in the right-hand column (see Figure 5.16).**

The new color appears in the Sample box, as shown in Figure 5.16.

Figure 5.16
The Format Data Series dialog box.

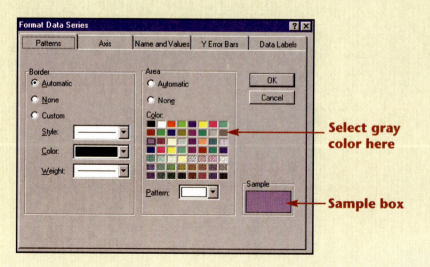

Lesson 4: Enhancing a Chart

7 Choose OK.

The dialog box closes and the new color appears in the chart. Now you want to change the number format of the labels on the Y-axis to show dollars with two decimal places.

8 Double-click any one of the dollar amounts on the Y-axis of the chart.

The Format Axis dialog box appears.

9 Select the Number tab.

The Number tab and its options appear (see Figure 5.17).

Figure 5.17
The Number options of the Format Axis dialog box.

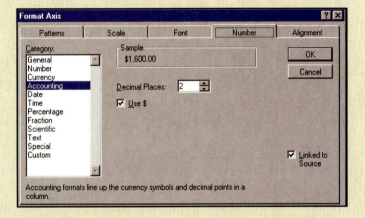

10 Select the Accounting Category in the Decimal Places text box, type 2, and then choose OK.

This selects a format with two decimal places. Excel displays two decimal places in the dollar values on the Y-axis. Your chart should now resemble the one shown in Figure 5.18. Keep the Expenses worksheet file open. You use it in the next lesson to learn how to print a worksheet that includes a chart.

continues

Project 5 Using Charts and Maps

To Enhance a Chart (continued)

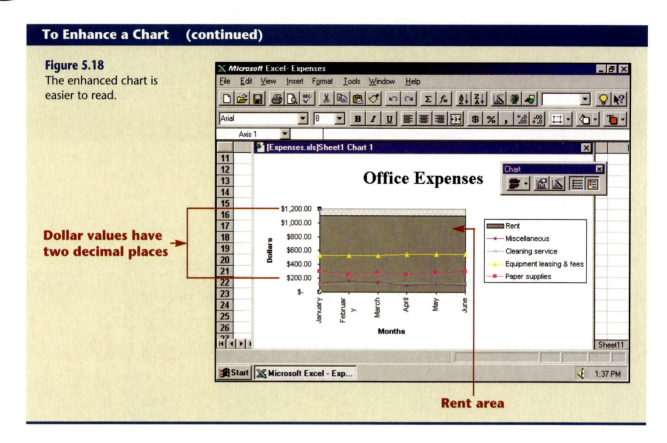

Figure 5.18
The enhanced chart is easier to read.

Dollar values have two decimal places

Rent area

You can move a selected chart box by dragging it to a new location. You can also resize a selected chart by positioning the mouse pointer over any one of the chart box handles until the pointer changes to a four-headed arrow. Drag the handle away from the center of the chart box to enlarge the box and toward the center of the box to reduce it.

When you drag a handle on the middle of one side of the box, you change the size horizontally or vertically. When you drag a corner handle, you change both the vertical and horizontal dimensions at the same time.

If you want to delete a chart, simply select the chart and press Del.

Lesson 5: Printing a Chart

Unless you want to carry around a laptop computer to show your work on-screen, you need to be able to print your worksheets.

Printing lets you view the worksheets you have created, even when you are away from your computer. A printed copy of a chart combined with the worksheet data makes a very effective presentation. Now try printing the entire Expenses workbook file, including the chart.

Lesson 5: Printing a Chart

To Print a Chart

❶ In the Expenses worksheet, close the Chart window and click anywhere outside the chart.

This ensures that no range in the worksheet is selected, not even the chart.

❷ Open the File menu and choose Page Setup.

The Page Setup dialog box appears (see Figure 5.19). Use this dialog box to adjust the page setup before you print your worksheet. This dialog box provides a wide range of options from which you can choose to customize your printed worksheet. For this example, you want to change the margins, header, and footer for the printed worksheet.

Figure 5.19
The Page Setup dialog box.

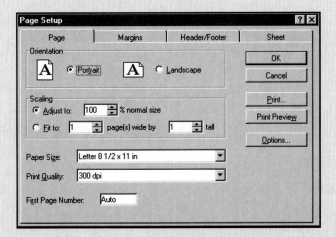

❸ In the Page Setup dialog click the Header/Footer tab.

The Header and Footer options enable you to specify information to print in the header and footer area of each page. You can choose from predefined headers and footers, or you can create your own.

❹ Click the drop-down arrow next to the Header text box and select Prepared by {YOUR NAME} MM/DD/YY, Page 1.

This header will print the words Prepared by, followed by your name and today's date in the center of the header and the page number on the right side of the header.

❺ Click the drop-down arrow next to the Footer text box and select Expenses.

This footer prints the current file name in the center of the footer area.

❻ Click the Margins tab in the Page Setup dialog box.

This displays the Margins options.

continues

To Print a Chart (continued)

7 **In the Top text box, click the up arrow twice.**

This changes the top margin to 1.5.

8 **In the Bottom text box, click the down arrow once.**

This changes the bottom margin to 0.75. You have now finished setting up the worksheet page for printing. Now preview the page to make sure it is the way you want it to print.

9 **Click the Print Preview button in the Page Setup dialog box.**

Excel closes the Page Setup dialog box, makes the changes you requested to the page setup, and displays the Print Preview window, as shown in Figure 5.20. In Print Preview, you can see the worksheet as it will look when you print it. You can also open the Print Preview window by clicking the Print Preview button on the Standard toolbar when the Page Setup dialog box isn't open. Everything looks the way you want it to, so you are ready to print.

Figure 5.20
Print Preview shows you the page as it will print, including the chart.

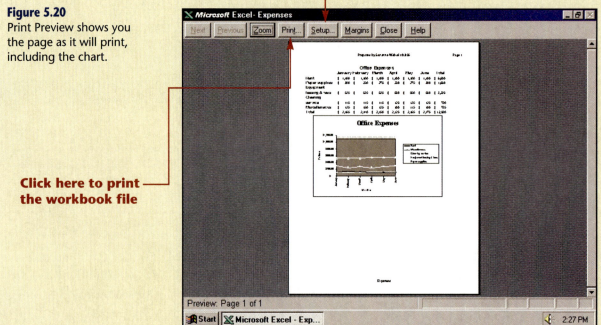

Click here to open the Page Setup dialog box

Click here to print the workbook file

10 **Click the Print button on the Print Preview toolbar.**

Print Preview closes and the Print dialog box appears.

11 **In the Copies text box, change the number of copies to 2, and then choose OK.**

Lesson 6: Creating a Map

Excel prints two copies of the worksheet, including the chart. When you are done printing, save and close the Expenses workbook file. In Lesson 7, you learn how to create a map using data in a different workbook file.

You can print just a chart in Excel without printing the entire worksheet. Simply select the chart, then choose **P**rint from the **F**ile menu to open the Print dialog box. Click the **S**election option button in the Print range area, then choose OK.

If you want to leave additional space between the chart and the worksheet data, simply select the chart and drag it down a few rows. Remember to deselect the chart before printing.

Lesson 6: Creating a Map

Maps are useful for charting information that is defined by state, country, or province. Maps are not one of Excel's built-in chart types; rather, they are a separate feature of Excel. Maps can help you visualize your worksheet information geographically. In this lesson, you compare how many company offices are located in different states in the U.S. By creating a map, you can see where most of the offices are located.

Try creating a map now using the sample worksheet provided.

To Create a Map

❶ Open the file Proj0502 and save it as SiteMap.

❷ Select the range A3:B19.

This selects all the data in the worksheet so that the information can be used to create your map.

❸ Click the Map button on the Standard toolbar.

The mouse pointer changes to a crosshair, which you can use to specify where in the worksheet Excel should create the map.

❹ Click cell A21, then drag the mouse pointer to cell G35.

When you release the mouse button, Excel begins creating the map. This may take a few seconds. Excel looks to see which map the data belongs in. If the data could fit in more than one map (which is the case in this example), the Multiple Maps Available dialog box appears, as shown in Figure 5.21.

continues

Project 5 Using Charts and Maps

To Create a Map (continued)

Figure 5.21
The Multiple Maps Available dialog box.

5 **Select United States, then choose OK.**

You may have to wait for several seconds while Excel composes the map. The map appears in the selected cells, along with the Data Map Control dialog box, as shown in Figure 5.22. The map is inserted in a frame, which you can use to resize and move the map. You can use the Data Map Control dialog box to change some formatting characteristics of the map. Because the shading values in the map are not easy to discern, try changing the colors of the map now.

Figure 5.22
The map showing the states in which offices are located.

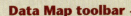

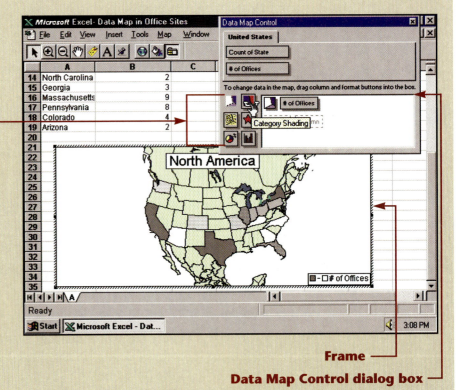

If you have problems...

If the Data Map Control dialog box is covering the map so you cannot see it, simply drag the dialog box out of the way. You can open and close the dialog box by using the Data Map Control Box button on the Data Map toolbar.

Lesson 6: Creating a Map

E-131

6 **In the Data Map Control dialog box, drag the Category shading button on to the # of Offices button, as shown in Figure 5.23.**

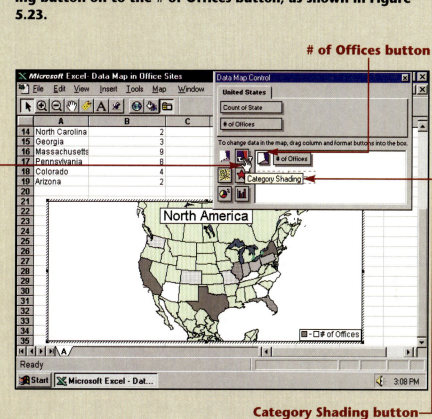

Figure 5.23
Use the Data Map Control dialog box to change the format of the map.

When you release the mouse button, Excel redraws the map, adding color to indicate the number of offices in each state, as shown in Figure 5.24. (Close the Data Map Control dialog box to see the map clearly.) By default, however, Excel displays the map's legend in a compact format, which does not provide much information. Try expanding the legend now.

Figure 5.24
The location of offices is now clearly indicated by color, but the legend is too compact to be of any use in identifying the location of offices.

7 **Double-click the map legend.**

This selects the legend, and opens the Edit Legend dialog box, as shown in Figure 5.23.

continues

To Create a Map (continued)

Figure 5.25
The Edit Legend dialog box.

Click here to expand the map legend

8 **Click in the Use Compact Format check box to deselect it, then choose OK.**

Excel redraws the map to expand the legend, as shown in Figure 5.26. You can now use the colors and the numbers in the legend to identify which part of the country has the greatest number of offices (the number identifies the number of offices in each state by color; the number in parentheses identifies how may states have that number of offices), and you decide to focus your research on the states surrounding Ohio. Try zooming in on that area now.

Figure 5.26
The map with an expanded legend.

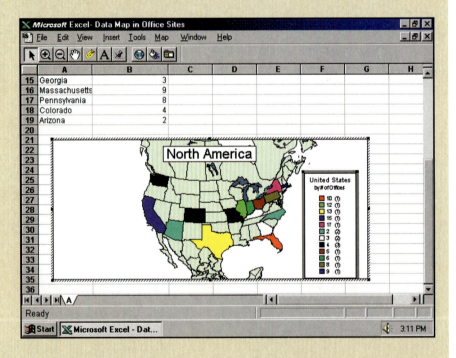

9 **Click the Zoom In button on the Data Map toolbar, then click Ohio in the map.**

Excel redraws the map, zooming in on the Ohio region. Now change the title of the map.

Lesson 6: Creating a Map

> **If you have problems...**
>
> If you are unhappy with the view, use the Zoom Out button to zoom out to a wider view, or return to the previous view by opening the **V**iew menu and choosing **P**revious Map. To view the entire map, choose **V**iew, **E**ntire Map.

10 **Click the Select Objects button on the Data Map toolbar, then double-click the map's title.**

This selects the map's title, and positions the insertion point in the text so that you can enter and edit the title text. You can change the text as well as the text attributes, including font, font size, and font style.

11 **Change the text to Office Locations, then press ↵Enter.**

This changes the map's title. While the title is selected, you can drag it to a new location on the map or resize it so that it doesn't cover any of the target states.

12 **Drag the map title to the upper left corner of the map.**

You have now completed the map. Click anywhere outside the map frame to deselect it. The map should now look similar to the one in Figure 5.27. Save your work. If requested by your instructor, print two copies. Then close the worksheet.

If you have completed your session on the computer, exit Excel and Windows 95 before turning off your computer. Otherwise, continue with the "Applying Your Skills" case studies at the end of this project.

Figure 5.27
The completed map.

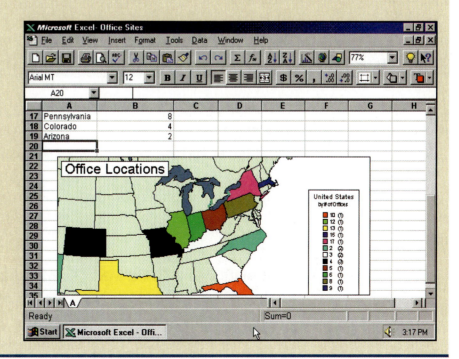

When creating a map, you need to have two columns of data. The first column contains the name of the region or state. You can use abbreviations—such as WV, TN, NC, and so on—or you can use the state's full name. The second column contains the worksheet information. The data in the second column is represented on the map by colors and/or patterns.

As with the elements in a chart, you can right-click elements in a map to open a shortcut menu. You can use the commands on the shortcut menus to quickly edit or enhance the parts of the map.

To print the worksheet with the map, choose **P**rint from the **F**ile menu, select options in the Print dialog box, and then choose OK. To print the map without printing the entire worksheet, click the map to select it, click the **S**election option button in the Print dialog box, then choose OK. You can change options, such as the header, footer, and margins, using the Page Setup dialog box, just as you do for all worksheets.

Project Summary

To	Do This
Start the ChartWizard	Click the ChartWizard button.
Edit a Chart	Double-click the chart.
Select a Chart	Click the chart.
Change a Chart Type	Choose a chart type from the Chart type drop-down list on the Chart toolbar.
Print a Chart	Select the chart, then click the Print button.
Create a Map	Click the Map button on the Standard toolbar.

Applying Your Skills

The following exercises enable you to practice the skills you have learned in this project. Take a few minutes to work through these exercises now.

Creating a Chart and Map Showing Mail Order Sales

In the past six months, you have tried to expand your business by adding a mail order catalog that you send to potential customers in the western United States. Create a chart and a map to show the sales for a mail order catalog business in the first quarter of 1996.

To Create a Chart and Map Showing Mail Order Sales

1. Open the file Proj0503 and save it as **MOSChart**.
2. Select the data for both columns and create a chart. Think about which type of chart will best show a comparison of the states in the mail order channel. Don't forget to add a title to the chart.
3. Select the data for both columns and create a map.

4. Experiment with some of the map features to enhance the map. For example, change the colors on the map, and expand the legend.

5. Change the map title to **Mail Order Sales**. Try editing the font of the title text.

6. Save your work. If requested by your instructor, print two copies before closing the file.

Comparing Expenses Using a Chart

Use the Master Budget worksheet to create a pie chart that compares how much you spend on various types of school expenses. Your tuition each semester is determined by the university, but you can try to manage other costs. Use the chart to see how changes in how much you spend on the Books–Additional category affects the makeup of the total amount.

To Compare Expenses Using a Chart

1. Open the file Proj0504 and save it as **Charting Expenses**.

2. Create a chart using the following expense data for the Spring 1995 semester: Books–Main subjects; Books–Additional; Supplies–General; Supplies–Lab; and Lab Fees.

3. Now change the chart type so that you can compare how the various types of expenses contribute to your total expenses for the semester. (*Tip*: Refer to Table 5.1.)

4. What happens to the worksheet and the chart when you decrease the amount in the worksheet for Books–Additional from $85 to $25?

5. What happens to the worksheet and the chart when you drastically increase the amount in the worksheet for Books–Additional to $475?

6. Save your work. If requested by your instructor, print two copies of the worksheet with the increased expense for Books–Additional. Then close the file.

Creating a Map of the Home States of Rollerblading Club Members

In an effort to show prospective club members how diverse the rollerblading club is, you decide to create a map showing the home states of all current members.

To Create the Map

1. Open Proj0505 and save it as **Membership Map.**

2. Use the data provided to create a map.

3. Zoom in on the target area.

4. Format the map to clearly show from which states most club members come. For example, make use of the legend, show the states in color, and use titles and text.

5. Save the worksheet. If requested by your instructor, print two copies. Then close it.

Checking Your Skills

True/False

For each of the following, check *T* or *F* to indicate whether the statement is true or false.

__T __F **1.** Use the same naming rules for sheets as you would for cells and ranges.

__T __F **2.** You can add up to 239 sheets to one file, if your computer's memory can handle it.

__T __F **3.** A good example of a 3D worksheet file is when you view three worksheets tiled on-screen.

__T __F **4.** To move to the first cell of the current sheet of a multiple worksheet file, press Ctrl+Home.

__T __F **5.** When referencing multiple sheets, you can use the sheet letter in the formula.

Multiple Choice

Circle the letter of the correct answer for each of the following.

1. Which of the following formulas does *not* contain a valid reference in a multiple worksheet file?

   a. +B!B12+B!B14+C!A10

   b. =SUM(A!A4;B!A4;C!A4)

   c. =AVG(A12+A14,C!B12+C!B14)

   d. =A!A12*C!A12

2. Which of the following statements is false?

   a. You can copy data from Sheet1 to Sheet2 and Sheet3.

   b. You can move data from one sheet to the Clipboard, move to another sheet, and then paste the data from the Clipboard to the new sheet.

   c. You can move data on the same sheet.

   d. You can move data from Sheet1 to the Clipboard, copy data from Sheet2 to Sheet3, and then paste the data from Sheet1 to Sheet3.

3. Which of the following is a valid sheet name?

   a. Expenses for 1994

   b. *.PAT EXPENSES

   c. AB:122

   d. School?

4. Which of the following is *not* a valid keyboard shortcut for moving around in multiple worksheets?

   a. Ctrl+PgDn

   b. Ctrl+Home

   c. Ctrl+PgUp

   d. End+Ctrl+Home

5. Excel workbooks have _____ worksheet files when you open a new workbook file.

   a. one

   b. five

   c. sixteen

   d. ten

Completion

In the blank provided, write the correct answer for each of the following statements.

1. If three worksheets are on-screen at the same time, you can press _____ to move from worksheet to worksheet.

2. When referencing multiple sheets in a formula, you should include the _____ and the cell references in the address.

3. A shortcut for deleting a worksheet is to activate it and _____ the sheet's tab to bring up the shortcut menu; then choose Delete.

4. If Sheet3 is active, you can press _____ to move to Sheet2.

5. You can rename a worksheet by _____ the sheet tab.

Project 6

Managing Data

Creating an Address Database

In this project, you learn how to
- Name a List
- Add Records
- Sort Records
- Find and Delete Records
- Extract Records Using AutoFilter

Why Would I Do This?

The purpose of creating a *database* (called a *list* in Excel for Windows) is to organize the information it contains and to view selected parts of the information. A good example of a database is a phone book, in which information is organized by city and then by name. To see only a portion of the phone book, you turn pages and scan columns of names arranged alphabetically. To see only part of a list in Excel, you use commands.

Computer databases provide you with a powerful way to organize and search for information. In this project, you learn to use a sample database of names, company names, addresses, and phone numbers. A simple Excel list, such as the one in this project, can make it much easier to stay in contact with business associates.

Lesson 1: Naming a List

A list in Excel is a special kind of worksheet in which column heads are *fields* and each row of the worksheet is a *record*. To continue with the phone book example, "Last Name" is one field, "First Name" is another field, "Address" is another field, and so on. A record consists of the set of information for one person: the person's first name, last name, address, and phone number. (See the upcoming Jargon Watch for more information about the database terminology used in this lesson.)

Each workbook file can contain more than one list, just as it can contain more than one worksheet, or you can create one workbook for each list. Each list can be on a separate worksheet or in separate ranges in a single worksheet.

Before you start to create a list, give some thought to the structure you want. Think about what you want to do with the information in the list; planning in advance can prevent you from having to move and insert columns later.

Follow these rules when creating a list in Excel:

- ▶ The field names must be in a single row.
- ▶ The field names must consist of text, not numbers. (If a field name contains a number, the entire name must be enclosed in quotation marks in order for Excel to interpret the name as text.) A field name can contain spaces.
- ▶ The field names must be unique.
- ▶ A list should not contain blank columns; it's best not to have blank rows either. Don't leave a blank row between the row of field names and the first data record.
- ▶ Every record must have the same fields, but you don't have to enter data into all the fields for every record. If the information is not available, you can leave some of the columns in a record empty.

Lesson 1: Naming a List   E-141

Now that you know a little about how lists are created in Excel, try opening a worksheet file that already contains information suitable for a list, then naming the list in the file. As a list grows, referring to the collection of data by name will be much easier than trying to remember the first and last cells of the list.

To Name a List

1 **Open the file Proj0601 and save it as Address Book.**

This is a sample database of business associates that you will use throughout this project (see Figure 6.1). Notice that no empty rows or columns are within the worksheet. The column headings in row 1, such as First Name and Last Name, are the field names for the list.

Figure 6.1
In Excel, a list of names and addresses can be used as an address database.

2 **Select the entire list, including the field names (cells A1:I21).**

Naming a list is similar to naming any range of cells. First, you must select the range you want to name—in this case, the entire list.

3 **Open the Insert menu, move the mouse pointer to the Name command, then choose Define from the nested menu that appears.**

The Define Name dialog box appears, as shown in Figure 6.2.

continues

To Name a List (continued)

Figure 6.2
Name a list in the Define Name dialog box.

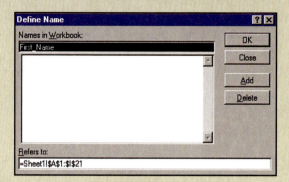

4 In the Names in Workbook text box, type **Address**, and then choose OK.

You have now named the database list so that you can easily refer to it in your work. Save the Address Book file and keep it open to use in the next lesson.

Jargon Watch

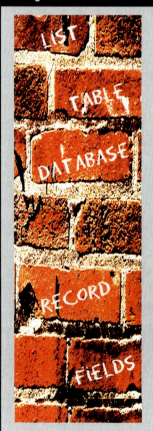

You may already know that **databases** can also be a separate type of application software for personal computers. Applications such as Access, Paradox, and dBASE are powerful programs used by all types of organizations and businesses. Many databases used in business and scientific research are so large and complex that they must run on mainframe computers.

In general terms, however, you can think of a database as an organized collection of related information—whether the information takes the form of a phone book, a recipe card file, or a disk file in a computer program.

Many database programs use what's called a **table** to organize the information contained in a database file. In Excel, this concept is referred to as a **list**, which is simply a worksheet of columns and rows.

Each collection of related information in a database is called a **record**. For example, in your address database from Lesson 1, each name and its accompanying address, city, state, Zip code, and phone number is considered a record. A single database list can contain thousands of records; the only real limitation is the amount of memory on the computer holding the information.

Each record in a database contains several parts, or **fields**. For example, in the personal address database, the first name is a field, the last name is a field, the address is a field, the city is a field, and so on. Each field must have a designated field name so that it is easy to identify when used in the program. A field name can consist of up to 255 characters, but as a rule you should keep field names brief and descriptive of the field's contents.

Lesson 2: Adding Records

After the initial database list is created, you may decide to add records to the list. You can simply type the new data into the rows at the end of the list, or you can use Excel's data form feature to add a number of records all at once.

A *data form* is basically a dialog box that shows all the fields in one data record. The data form presents an organized view of the data and makes data entry easier and more accurate. The data form is especially useful with much larger databases than the sample address database used in this project.

Try adding records to the address database now.

Data form
A dialog box that displays only one row of your list—in other words, one record. Column headings appear as field labels. You can enter data, or work with existing data using a data form.

To Add Records

❶ In the Address Book worksheet, select any cell in the list, then open the Data menu and choose Form.

A data form dialog box opens, displaying the contents of the first record in the Address list.

❷ Click the New button in the data form dialog box.

A new, blank form appears, as shown in Figure 6.3. You enter data for new records in the blank form.

Figure 6.3
A blank data form.

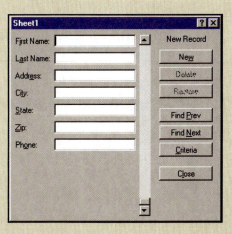

❸ Type Mohammed in the First Name field text box, and then press Tab.

This enters the data into the First Name field of a new data record. Pressing Tab moves the insertion point to the next field text box.

❹ Type Khalili in the Last Name field text box, and then press Tab.

This enters the data into the Last Name field of the data record.

continues

To Add Records (continued)

❺ Continue entering the record using the following data: Company: Gadgets, Inc.; Title: Sales Manager; Address field: 526 Lynn St; City field: Ithaca; State field: NY; Zip field: 14850; and Phone field: 607-555-3421.

Don't forget to press Tab to move from one field to the next.

❻ Press ↵Enter after typing all the field information.

This enters the new data record into the list, and displays a new blank form, which you can use to continue adding records. Now add three more records to the address database.

❼ Enter the following record data:

> Natalie, Burnett, Style Systems, V.P. Marketing, 21 Magnolia St, Battle Creek, MI, 49017, 616-555-2394
>
> Wendell, Feldman, Baker Computing, Dir. Sales, 270 West Limestone St, Orem, UT, 84057, 801-555-3002
>
> Eve, Shaw, Baker Computing, Sales Rep., 1170 North 17th St, Orem, UT, 84057, 801-555-8202

Remember to press Tab to move from field to field, and press ↵Enter to display a new, blank data form.

❽ Click the Close button in the Data Form dialog box.

This clears the dialog box from the screen and displays the address list. Scroll down in the list to see the new records, as shown in Figure 6.4. Now you need to extend the range name for your list to encompass the new records.

Figure 6.4
The new records are added to the bottom of the list.

Lesson 3: Sorting Records

9 **Select the entire list, including field names.**

You must redefine the list name to include the new records.

10 **Open the Insert menu, move the mouse pointer to the Name command, and choose Define.**

The Define Name dialog box appears.

11 **Select the list name Address in the Names in Workbook list box.**

The list name (Address) appears in the Names in Workbook text box (see Figure 6.5).

Figure 6.5
Redefine the Address list to include the new records.

12 **In the Refers to text box, change the last cell reference from row 21 to row 25, then choose OK.**

This redefines the Address list to include the records you just added. Save your work and keep the Address Book worksheet open to use in the next lesson.

Lesson 3: Sorting Records

To *sort* a list means to rearrange the list in a particular order. The sort order is determined by the *sort fields* you set for Excel. The sort fields are simply the fields you want Excel to use in sorting.

Sort
A function that rearranges the data in a list so it appears in alphabetical or numerical order.

You can also choose the kind of order you want Excel to follow in sorting the field. For example, in your address database, you can tell Excel to sort the Company field in ascending alphabetical order (that is, from A to Z), or in descending alphabetical order (that is, from Z to A).

Sort fields
Fields used to determine the order in which a list is sorted.

What if you have more than one person working at the same company? You can use additional sort fields to break ties; in this case, you can use the last name as a second field to sort, or perhaps the title field.

Try sorting records in your list now.

To Sort Records

❶ In the Address Book worksheet, select the entire list (cells A1:I25) if it isn't already selected.

This selects the records you want to sort.

❷ Open the Data menu and choose Sort.

The Sort dialog box appears, as shown in Figure 6.6. The **S**ort By text box is selected with the name of the first field displayed.

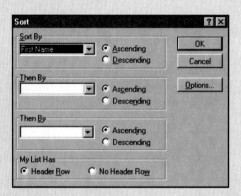

Figure 6.6
The Sort dialog box.

❸ In the My List Has box at the bottom of the Sort dialog box, make sure that the Header Row option button is selected.

This confirms that you have included the field names in the first row in the sorting range. Excel now knows to leave the first row out of the sort.

❹ Type City in the Sort By text box, and then choose OK.

Excel sorts the records by city in ascending alphabetical order, as shown in Figure 6.7. Ascending order is the default in the Sort dialog box. You can also choose to sort in descending order. Notice that the list records remain selected after the sort is performed. Now try resorting the list by Company.

❺ With the records for cells A1 through I25 still selected, open the Data menu and choose Sort.

The Sort dialog box appears again. Notice that City appears selected in the **S**ort By text box.

❻ Click the drop-down arrow next to the Sort By text box, and select Company from the drop-down list of field names that appears.

This enters Company in the **S**ort By text box, telling Excel you want to sort the records according to the data in the Company field. However, because you know some of your records have the same data in the Company field, you also want to sort the list by Last Name.

Lesson 3: Sorting Records E–147

Figure 6.7
Records are sorted alphabetically according to the data in the City field.

Sort field

7 **Click the drop-down arrow next to the first Then By text box, and select Last Name from the drop-down list of field names.**

Now you have added a second sort field—Last Name (see Figure 6.8). Excel will first sort by Company and then by Last Name.

Figure 6.8
You can sort a list using up to three sort fields.

First sort field

Second sort field

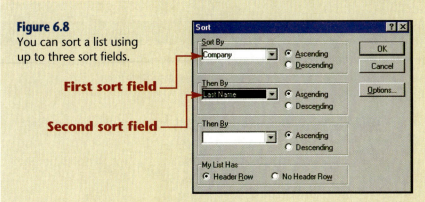

8 **Choose OK.**

Excel closes the dialog box and sorts the records. You may want to click a cell outside the range to deselect the list. Notice that the records have been alphabetized by company name, and in cases where there is more than one record per company, the records are further alphabetized by Last Name, as shown in Figure 6.9.

continues

To Sort Records (continued)

Figure 6.9
Records in the list are sorted alphabetically by Company Name, then by Last Name.

Sort Ascending

Sort Descending

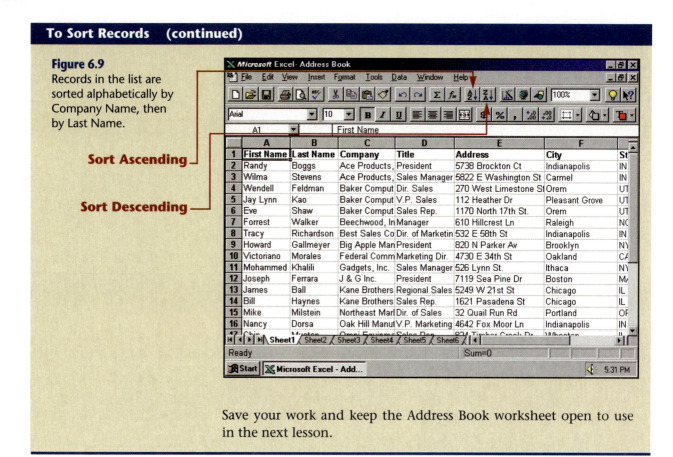

Save your work and keep the Address Book worksheet open to use in the next lesson.

If you have problems...

Be careful when selecting the data to sort. If you select only a column or two of data, Excel sorts only the selected data. Therefore, columns that aren't selected are not included in the sort.

If you selected only the Company Name and Last Name fields when sorting, you may find addresses and phone numbers paired with the wrong names. To reverse the sort, click the Undo button before performing any other action.

It's always a good idea to save your file before you perform a sort. If you make an error in sorting, you can close the file without saving, open the original file, and then try again.

To quickly sort a list by the data entered in the first field, click the Sort Ascending or Sort Descending buttons on the Standard toolbar.

Lesson 4: Finding and Deleting Records

One of the most useful functions of working with lists is using search criteria to find specific records. Using the Excel criteria data form to find specific records saves a great deal of time when you are working with dozens of records. For example, you can use search criteria to find every person in your list with a particular job title name.

Search Criteria
A defined pattern or detail used to find matching records.

You can also delete specific records in a list by using *search criteria* to find the records, then deleting them. For example, you can choose to delete all records containing a particular last name or all records containing a particular state. Be careful when deleting records; you can accidentally delete records that you need.

Try finding and deleting specific records in your list now.

To Find and Delete Records

1 **In the Address Book worksheet, click any cell in the list. Open the Data menu and choose Form.**

A data form appears containing the data from the current record.

2 **Click the Criteria button in the Data Form dialog box.**

A blank criteria data form appears, as shown in Figure 6.10. You use the criteria data form to specify the records you want to find. Now specify criteria to find and then delete all the records for people working at Baker Computing.

Figure 6.10
A blank Criteria data form.

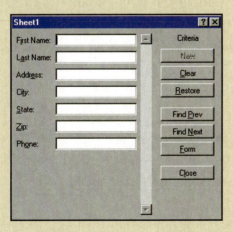

3 **Click in the Company text box and type Baker Computing.**

This tells Excel to look through the Company field in every record to find the data Baker Computing.

4 **Click the Find Next button.**

Excel begins the search, and displays the data form for the next record in the list that matches the specified criterion—meaning the

continues

To Find and Delete Records (continued)

next record from the company Baker Computing, as shown in Figure 6.11.

Figure 6.11
Excel displays a record that matches the criteria you entered.

Company field

5 Click the Delete button.

Excel displays a dialog box warning you that the record will be permanently deleted.

If you have problems...

Be careful when deleting records from your database. Once you choose OK in the warning dialog box, Excel deletes the record permanently. You can't retrieve the deleted record using the **U**ndo command.

6 Choose OK.

Excel deletes the record, and displays the data form for the next record in the database, whether or not it matches the search criteria (in this case it does, because the records are sorted by company name). Now continue your search using the criteria data form to delete the rest of the records from Baker Computing.

7 Click the Find Next button.

Again, Excel displays the next record that matches the specified criteria.

8 Click the Delete button, and then choose OK in the warning box.

Excel deletes the record. Repeat the steps to find and delete any additional records from Baker Computing. When no further records in the list match the criteria, Excel beeps.

9 Click the Close button in the data form dialog box.

This clears the dialog box and displays the Address Book worksheet. Save your work and keep the worksheet open. In the next lesson, you use Excel's AutoFilter to extract records from the database.

Lesson 5: Extracting Records Using AutoFilter

If you want to find records that match complex criteria, you can use Excel's AutoFilter feature. With a *filter*, you set criteria to specify which records you want displayed in the list. Filtering does not delete the records that don't match your criteria; it just hides them until you want to display them again.

Filter
A method for controlling which records are extracted from the database and displayed in the worksheet.

In this lesson, for example, assume that you want to send a letter to everyone in your database who works at a specific company in Chicago or Indianapolis, telling them that you will be visiting those cities soon and would like to meet. You can use the AutoFilter to extract all the records for those cities from the original list.

When you use a large database with hundreds of records, filtering data enables you to work with a more manageable set of records and fields. Always save your file before you filter data. If you have a problem extracting the records, you can close the file and revert to the saved version of the original data. Try extracting records using AutoFilter and your address database now.

To Extract Records Using AutoFilter

❶ In the Address Book worksheet, click in any cell in the list.

This tells Excel that you want to use AutoFilter to find records in the list. You do not have to select the entire list.

❷ Open the Data menu, move the mouse pointer to the Filter command and choose AutoFilter from the nested menu.

Filter arrows appear next to each of the field names in the list, as shown in Figure 6.12. You specify which field you want to use for filtering by using the filter arrow in that field. In this case, you want to filter records based on the City field.

Figure 6.12
The address list when AutoFilter is in use.

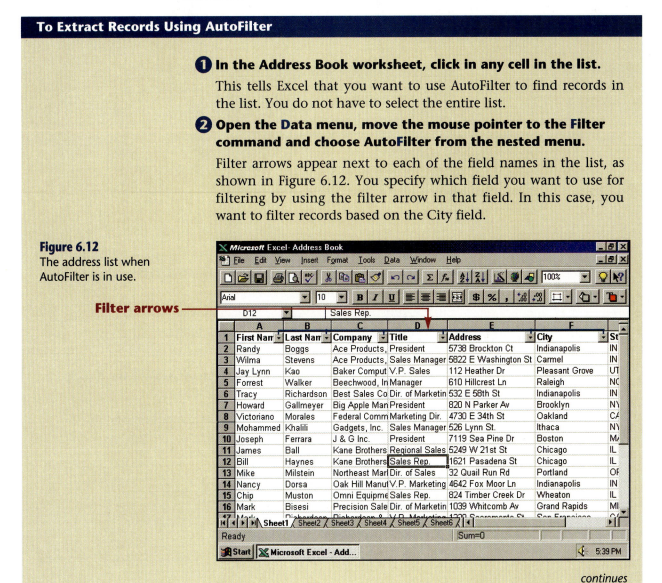

continues

To Extract Records Using AutoFilter (continued)

4 **Click the filter arrow in cell F1.**

A drop-down list of filtering criteria appears under the arrow. (All), (Top Ten...), and (Custom...) are always displayed at the top of the list. (All), the default, shows all the records without using the field as a filter. Choose (All) when you want to remove any filtering criteria already in use for a field.(Top Ten...) lets you filter records according to the highest or lowest values in the list. (Custom...) lets you specify multiple selection criteria to use for filtering the field.

5 **From the drop-down list, select (Custom...).**

The Custom AutoFilter dialog box appears (see Figure 6.13). This is where you specify the criteria that Excel uses to extract records from the database. You can specify two criteria, using two operators. *Operators* tell Excel the type of comparison you want to use. For example, the = operator means to match the criteria exactly, and the < operator means to find records where the data is less than the specified criteria. Notice that = appears in the first operator text box by default.

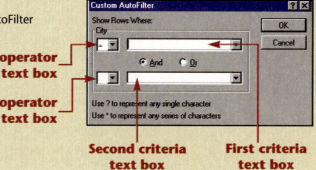

Figure 6.13
The Custom AutoFilter dialog box.

First operator text box
Second operator text box
Second criteria text box
First criteria text box

6 **Click the drop-down arrow next to the first criteria text box, and select Chicago.**

This establishes City = Chicago as the first filter criterion. Remember that you want to include records either from Chicago *or* from Indianapolis.

7 **Click the Or option button in the Custom AutoFilter dialog box.**

Next, you want to include Indianapolis in the criteria statement.

Lesson 5: Extracting Records Using AutoFilter

8 **Click the drop-down arrow next to the second operator text box.**

This displays the drop-down list of relational operators, as shown in Figure 6.14.

Figure 6.14
Specify the type of comparison by selecting an operator from the drop-down list.

← List of operators

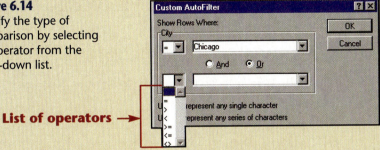

9 **Select the = operator.**

This tells Excel you want to find all records that match the specified criteria.

10 **Click the drop-down arrow next to the second criteria text box arrow, and select Indianapolis from the list of data entries that appears.**

Your dialog box should now resemble Figure 6.15. Make sure that the = relational operator appears in both Operator text boxes, and that the **O**r option is selected.

Figure 6.15
The completed Custom AutoFilter dialog box.

11 **Choose OK in the Custom AutoFilter dialog box.**

Excel extracts all records that match the specified criteria and displays them in the list, as shown in Figure 6.16. In this case, only records where the City field contains the data Chicago or Indianapolis are displayed. All other records are temporarily hidden. Notice that the filter arrow for the City field is colored blue to indicate that the City field has been used to filter data.

continues

To Extract Records Using AutoFilter (continued)

Figure 6.16
The extracted records for Chicago and Indianapolis are displayed.

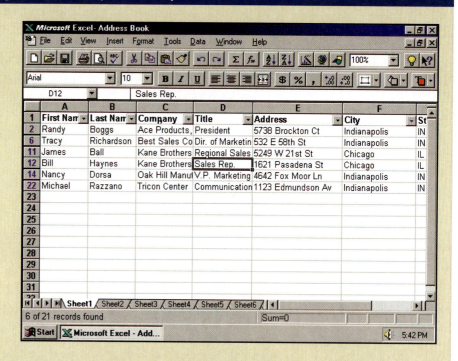

 Open the **D**ata menu, move the mouse pointer to the **F**ilter command and choose Auto**F**ilter from the nested menu that appears.

This turns off the AutoFilter feature, and all records in the list are again displayed. Notice that the filter arrows disappear. Save your work. If requested by your instructor, print two copies. Then close the worksheet.

If you have completed your session on the computer, exit Excel for Windows and Windows 95 before turning off the computer. Otherwise, continue with the "Applying Your Skills" section at the end of this project.

Removing all old filtering conditions before you set new filtering conditions is always a good idea. Otherwise, you may forget that you have previously set a filtering condition that is still affecting a more recent search. Choose **D**ata, **F**ilter, **S**how All to clear the preceding filters.

You can clear a filter from a single column by clicking the filter button for that column, and choosing **A**ll from the list. To turn off AutoFilter completely, simply choose **D**ata, **F**ilter, Auto**F**ilter.

Project Summary

To	Do This
Name a list	Select the list, choose **I**nsert, **N**ame, **D**efine, type the name in the Names in **W**orkbook text box in the Define Name dialog box, then choose OK.
Add records	Choose **D**ata, **F**orm, click Ne**w**, type data in the fields, press Tab to move from one field to the next.
Sort records according to the first field	Click the Sort Ascending or Sort Descending buttons on the Standard toolbar.
Find records	Choose **D**ata, **F**orm, click **C**riteria, type the data to find in the appropriate field, and click Find **N**ext.
Delete records	Find the record you want to delete and click **D**elete in the Data Form dialog box. Click OK in the warning dialog box.
Filter the list of records	Choose **D**ata, **F**ilter, then select the filter you want to use, or choose AutoFilter to create your own filter. Drop down the filtering criteria list in the field you want to filter and choose the the criteria you want to use, or choose Custom to specify your own filtering criteria.
Display all records	Choose **D**ata, **F**ilter, AutoFilter.

Applying Your Skills

The following exercises enable you to practice the skills you have learned in this project. Take a few minutes to work through these exercises now.

Creating the Inventory List

Use the product information provided to create an inventory list for keeping track of products.

To Create the Inventory List

1. Open the file Proj0602 and save it as **Products**.

2. Change the worksheet into a list by adding field names to the top of each column, as follows: Column A: **Product Name**; Column B: **Product Number**; Column C: **Unit Cost**; Column D: **In-Stock?**.

3. Sort the list alphabetically by product name so that you can easily find any product.

4. Extract a list of all products that are not in stock so that you know what needs to be reordered.

5. Save your list. If requested by your instructor, print two copies. Then close it.

Project 6 Managing Data

Using an Employee Database

With Excel's list feature, you can create an employee database that can help you track vital information about the staff of Sound Byte Music. You use this database to organize the work schedule and to analyze your staffing needs. In this case study, use the sort and AutoFilter features of Excel to organize the employee data and evaluate salaried, hourly, and commissioned staff.

To Use an Employee Database

1. Open the file Proj0603 and save it as **Employee List**.
2. Sort the list alphabetically in ascending order by three sort keys: last name, first name, and city.
3. Extract a list of commissioned employees.
4. Extract a list of hourly employees.
5. Extract a list of salaried employees who live in Oak Hill.
6. Save the file. If requested by your instructor, print two copies of the list, including all records. Then close it.

Creating a CD Collection Inventory

In Project 1, you created an inventory of your CD and cassette tape collection, including the title, artist, recording year, price, and other pertinent information. Now, using a similar worksheet, turn the data into a list to keep track of your music collection.

To Create the CD Inventory

1. Open the file Proj0604 and save it as **CD Inventory**.
2. Change the worksheet into a list by adding field names to the top of each column.
3. Sort the list alphabetically in ascending order by artist so that you can easily find any CD.
4. Extract a list of all titles that cost more than $12 or less than $10 so that you can track your most expensive and least expensive titles.
5. Save the file. If requested by your instructor, print two copies. Then close it.

Creating the Telephone List

For the rollerblading club, create a telephone list that you can use for notifying members of upcoming events and for contacting club officers, when necessary.

To Create the Telephone List

1. Open the file proj0605 and save it as **Phone List**.
2. Change the worksheet into a list by adding field names to the top of each column.
3. Sort the list alphabetically by members' last names in ascending order.

4. Extract a list of all club officers. (*Hint*: To do this, make use of the non blank option.)

5. Save the list. If requested by your instructor, print two copies. Then close it.

Checking Your Skills

True/False

For each of the following, check *T* or *F* to indicate whether the statement is true or false.

__T __F **1.** Naming a list is especially useful when you are working with a large amount of data.

__T __F **2.** Each collection of information in a list is divided into fields.

__T __F **3.** The field name identifies each record in a database table.

__T __F **4.** Excel can sort data using up to two fields.

__T __F **5.** An Excel list can be sorted only in ascending order.

Multiple Choice

Circle the letter of the correct answer for each of the following.

1. The _____ menu contains the command that lets you delete a record from a list.
   a. **F**ile
   b. **D**ata
   c. **T**ools
   d. none of the above

2. Which of the following does *not* describe a list?
   a. an organized collection of information
   b. data in a worksheet
   c. rows of fields
   d. related information

3. The _____ menu contains the command that enables you to define criteria.
   a. **E**dit
   b. **D**ata
   c. **S**election
   d. none of the above

4. Which option in the criteria list, displayed when you click a filter arrow, removes any filters for that field?

   a. (Blank)

   b. <>

   c. (All)

   d. none of the above

5. To find the records that match a search condition in the list, you click the _____ button in the data form.

   a. Search

   b. Seek

   c. Criteria

   d. none of the above

Completion

In the blank provided, write the correct answer for each of the following statements.

1. The best way to add records to an existing list is by using the Data _____.

2. When you have finished finding records using the AutoFilter, you can return to the worksheet by _____.

3. Each individual collection of related information in a database is called a _____.

4. To find records in a list where one criterion *or* the other is met, you use the _____.

5. The _____ names indicate the information contained in each record.

Project 7

Using Excel with Other Programs

Integrating Applications

In this project, you learn how to
- Switch among Applications
- Copy Data between Applications
- Link Data between Applications
- Work with Embedded Data

Project 7 Using Excel with Other Programs

Why Would I Do This?

While at your desk, you probably do several things in rapid succession: work on a paper, talk on the phone, and punch numbers into your calculator. Similarly, when you work on your computer, you may work for a few minutes on a document in a word processor, take a moment to update a worksheet, and then look up a phone number in a computer-based phone book.

Integration
Using two or more software applications together to create a single document.

Multitasking
The execution of more than one program at a time on a computer system.

One of the advantages of using software that runs under Windows 95 is that you have the capability to exchange data among various applications. In Windows 95, you can have more than one application running at once, so you can switch among applications as your need to work on different tasks occurs. You can display several applications' documents at the same time, if necessary, and you can exchange data among those documents. These features of Windows software, called *integration* or *multitasking*, make working with the computer easier and more intuitive.

Lesson 1: Switching among Applications

You can use the taskbar to switch among open applications and to start additional programs. The number of applications you can have open at one time is largely determined by the amount of available memory in your computer.

Try using the taskbar to switch among applications now.

To Switch among Applications

❶ In Excel, open the file Proj0701 and save it as Supply Expenses.

The worksheet includes a chart depicting a breakdown of office supply expenses.

❷ Click the Start button on the taskbar, and move the mouse pointer to the Programs command.

A list of programs installed on your computer appears, as shown in Figure 7.1.

Lesson 1: Switching among Applications

Figure 7.1
In Windows 95, you start programs by using the Start and Programs menus.

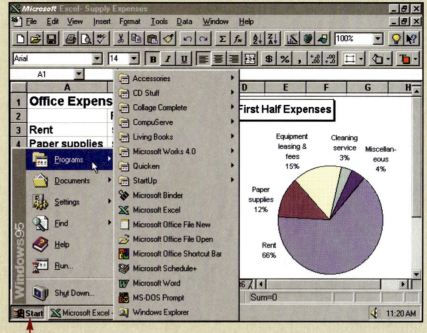

Start button

If you have problems...

Microsoft Word was chosen for this example because it is a popular word processing program that is widely available. If you cannot find Microsoft Word in your **P**rograms menu, or if you have a different version of Microsoft Word installed, check with your instructor for information about what to do in this project. Your instructor may have you use a different word processing application to complete the lessons in this project.

Don't worry if you have never used Word or any other word processing software before. The instructions in this project tell you exactly what to do. Remember, just about everything you do with Excel and Word in this project can be done using other Windows 95 applications. However, if you are using a different word processing application, the steps you use to complete the lessons may be slightly different.

❸ Click Microsoft Word on the Programs nested menu.

Microsoft Word for Windows 95 opens, as shown in Figure 7.2; Excel remains open and moves to the background. Notice that a button for Microsoft Word has been added to the taskbar. Microsoft Word is a word processing application often used in conjunction with Excel.

continues

Project 7 Using Excel with Other Programs

To Switch among Applications (continued)

Figure 7.2
In this project, you integrate Word documents with Excel documents.

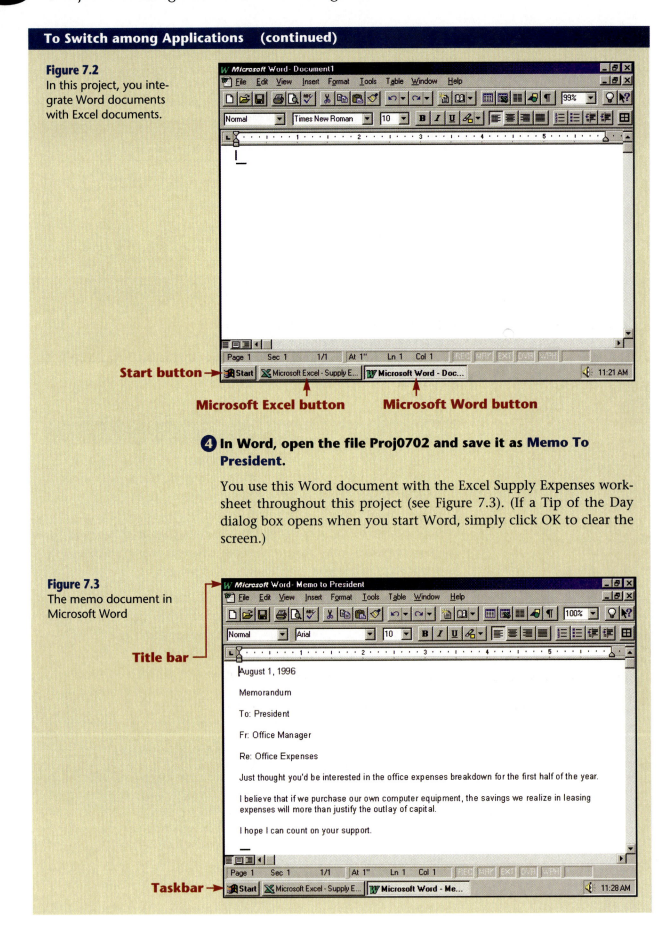

4 **In Word, open the file Proj0702 and save it as Memo To President.**

You use this Word document with the Excel Supply Expenses worksheet throughout this project (see Figure 7.3). (If a Tip of the Day dialog box opens when you start Word, simply click OK to clear the screen.)

Figure 7.3
The memo document in Microsoft Word

Lesson 2: Copying Data between Applications

> **5 Click the Microsoft Excel button on the taskbar.**
>
> This switches you back to Excel. Word remains open, running in the background. Keep all these documents and applications open. In Lesson 2, you learn how to copy data from one application to another.

Another quick way to switch among open applications is to press and hold down Alt as you press Tab. Each time you press Tab, the name of the next open application appears. When you see the name of the application you want to use, release both keys.

If you are distracted by an open application visible on the desktop behind the active application, maximize the active application to fill the desktop. If you want to switch to the application in the background, use the taskbar.

If you are using a suite of application programs, such as Microsoft Office, you can use the toolbar included with the suite to switch among programs. The toolbar usually appears in the title bar of the active applications, and it displays one button for each application in the suite. Click the application button to open or switch to a different application.

Microsoft Office is a collection of several Microsoft applications, sold in one package. Microsoft Office usually includes Excel, Word, PowerPoint (a presentation graphics software package), and Access (a database program). Microsoft Office also includes special features such as the application toolbar designed to make integration, or working with other Microsoft applications, easier.

If you have problems...

If you find that your system is slow or locking up, you may have opened a program twice instead of simply switching to it. From the **P**rograms menu you can open a program that is already running. From the taskbar, you cannot open an application that is already running.

If you accidentally open an application that is already open, Windows slows down considerably and may even lock up. To avoid this problem, just check the taskbar before opening new applications to make sure the program is not already running.

Lesson 2: Copying Data between Applications

It's easy to copy information from one application to another. This saves you from having to retype data that you have already entered. For example, suppose that you want to include a chart from the Supply Expenses worksheet you created in a letter to your company's president. You can perform this task easily using the Windows Clipboard and task-switching capabilities.

Try copying a chart from an Excel worksheet to a letter in Word now.

To Copy Data between Applications

1 **In Excel, select the First Half Expenses chart in the Supply Expenses worksheet.**

This is the chart you want to copy to the Memo to President.

2 **Click the Copy button on the Standard toolbar.**

The chart is copied to the Windows Clipboard. You can use the menu commands or the toolbar buttons to copy, cut, and paste data between applications.

3 **Click the Microsoft Word button on the taskbar.**

The Memo To President file that you opened earlier in this project should now be on-screen.

4 **Move the insertion point to the blank line at the end of the memo.**

This is where you want to insert the chart from Excel.

5 **Click the Paste button on the Standard toolbar.**

The chart is pasted from the Clipboard into the letter at the insertion point (see Figure 7.4). Save your work in the Memo To President Word file. Keep all the current files and applications open for the next lesson, where you learn how to link data between Excel and Word.

Figure 7.4
The First Half Expenses chart now appears in the Word document.

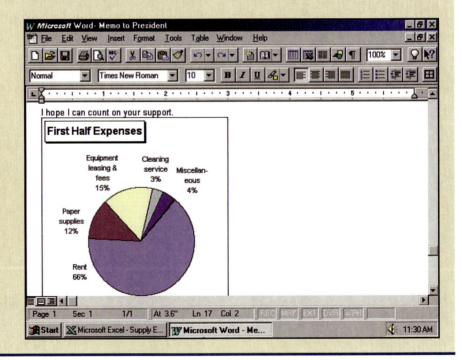

To move data from one application to another, use the **Cut** command or toolbar button rather than the **C**opy command. You can also display both worksheets on-screen at the same time, then select and drag the data you want to move from one worksheet to the other.

Lesson 3: Linking Data between Applications

The next level of sophistication in using Excel with other applications is to *link* data from Excel to a portion of a document in another program. For example, you can link a range of cells from the expense worksheet with the memo in Word so that if you change any values in the worksheet, the information in the Word document is updated automatically. Keep in mind however that you cannot edit the linked data in the Word document. (Look for the Jargon Watch later in this lesson for more information about the terminology of sharing information between applications).

Another benefit of linking Excel data to a Word document is that you can double-click the Excel data in Word and quickly switch to the Excel worksheet where you originally created the data. Unlike the copy you made of the chart in the previous lesson, linking the chart will update the document.

You create a link so that you don't have to remember to update the same information in two places—the original worksheet and its representation in the letter. Try linking data from the Supply Expenses worksheet to the Memo to President document now.

To Link Data between Applications

1 **In Word, click the chart you inserted previously in the Memo To President file, and then press** Del.

This selects the chart, then deletes it from the memo. You have decided to link a worksheet in the letter rather than use copied data that cannot be updated.

2 **Click the Excel button on the taskbar to switch to Excel.**

3 **Select cells A1 to H13 in the Supply Expenses worksheet.**

This is the worksheet data and chart that you want to link to your letter. Make sure that you select a range of cells that includes both the data and the associated chart.

4 **Click the Copy button.**

This copies the range and chart to the Windows Clipboard.

5 **Click the Microsoft Word button on the taskbar to switch to Word.**

Word is once again on-screen with the Memo To President document open.

6 **Move the insertion point to the blank line at the end of the document.**

This is where you want to insert the linked data from Excel.

7 **Choose Edit, Paste Special.**

The Paste Special dialog box appears (see Figure 7.5).

continues

To Link Data Between Applications (continued)

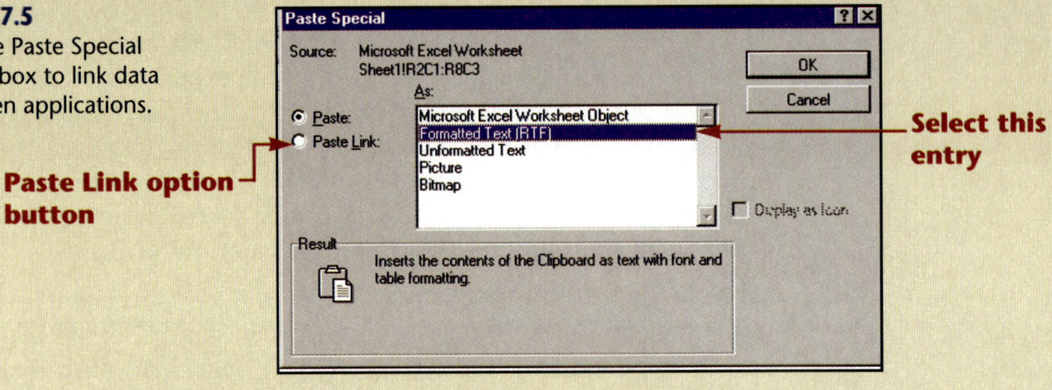

Figure 7.5
Use the Paste Special dialog box to link data between applications.

Paste Link option button

Select this entry

8. **Click the Paste Link option button.**

   This tells Word that you want to link the Excel data you are copying and pasting.

9. **Select Microsoft Excel Worksheet Object from the As data type list.**

   This tells Word that you want to paste a linked Excel worksheet object—that is, an actual Excel worksheet and chart that will be updated any time changes are made in the Supply Expenses worksheet. Notice that a description of the results of your selections appears in the Result area of the dialog box.

10. **Choose OK.**

    The Excel data is pasted into the memo, as shown in Figure 7.6. Now try changing a cell in the Excel worksheet to see how the linked data changes automatically.

Figure 7.6
Linked data from Excel is pasted into the Word document.

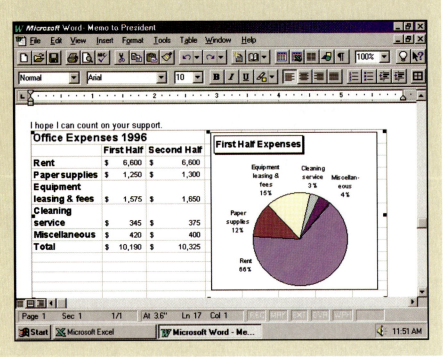

Lesson 3: Linking Data between Applications

⓫ **Double-click anywhere within the Excel data in the Word document.**

This switches back to Excel, with the Supply Expenses worksheet open.

⓬ **Change cell B5 in the worksheet to $575.00.**

This shows a possible decrease in the amount spent on computer equipment leasing. Make sure that you press Tab to update the change to the cell.

⓭ **Click the Microsoft Word button on the taskbar.**

Notice that the leasing and fees totals in the linked table data have been automatically updated, as shown in Figure 7.7. Also, notice that the changes are reflected in the chart.

Figure 7.7
The values changed in Excel are updated automatically in the linked table and in the chart in Word.

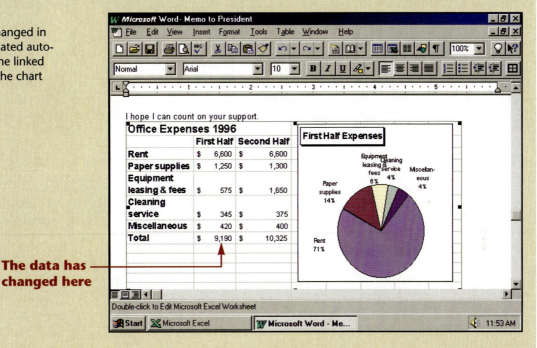

Save your work in both the Word document, Memo To President, and the Excel worksheet, Supply Expenses. Keep all the current files and applications open for the next lesson. In Lesson 4, you work directly with the Excel object embedded in Word.

If you have problems...

If the data does not update in Word, you may have just pasted instead of pasting a link. Go back to Excel and copy the spreadsheet again. Then switch to Word and make sure you choose **E**dit, Paste **S**pecial.

Also, if you change the location of either the source or the target document, the link between the two is broken. For example, if you move the target document to a different folder or disk, then change the data in the source, Excel cannot automatically update the link. You must repeat the link procedure in order to relink the data. If you plan to change the location of either document, you should consider simply copying the data from one to the other, or embedding the data, as described in Lesson 4.

Jargon Watch

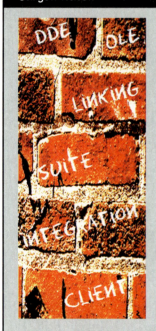

These days, **integration** is a hot buzz word in computing. For example, the Microsoft Office **suite** of applications are referred to as integrated because they share many features and standard commands.

The common Windows platform allows many Windows applications to easily share data. This feature of Windows goes by the catchy names **OLE**, which stands for **object linking and embedding**, and **DDE**, which stands for **dynamic data exchange**.

DDE uses **linking** to set up communication between two files so that when you update the **source** file, the **target** file in the link is automatically updated. Supply Expenses is the source file in Lesson 3, while Memo to President is the target file.

You can also call the two files in a linked relationship the **client** and the **server**. The server is the document in which the original text or data is located. The client is the document that reflects changes made in the server document.

OLE uses **embedding** to create an **object** in the client file. You use embedding in Lesson 4 to make changes in an Excel object that resides in Word. With embedding, the object is not linked in any way to the source file—you can edit the worksheet data using Excel functions, but the changes do not affect the original data.

Lesson 4: Working with Embedded Data

In Lesson 3, you linked an Excel worksheet object into the Word document, Memo To President. This is useful for keeping both the source and target documents current. However, there may be times when you want to keep the two separate—perhaps to experiment with the effects of possible changes in data—or when you may not have access to the source file once the target file has been created. In cases such as these, you want to embed the Excel worksheet object into the Word document, rather than linking it.

Lesson 4: Working with Embedded Data

Embedding the data enables you to edit the worksheet in the Word document without switching back to Excel. For example, if you want to take a quick look at the effect of decreased leasing costs on your expenses, you double-click the embedded Excel worksheet object and make changes directly to the worksheet—without ever leaving the memo you are writing. The original source file, Supply Expenses, is not affected by the change.

Try working with embedded worksheet data in your memo now.

To Work with Embedded Data

❶ In the Word file, Memo To President, click the Excel data and press Del.

This selects the data, then deletes it, severing the link between the two applications. Now try embedding an Excel worksheet object into the Word document.

❷ Click the Microsoft Excel button on the taskbar.

This switches you back to the Supply Expenses worksheet.

❸ Select cells A1 to H13 (if they are not already selected), and click the Copy button on the Standard toolbar.

This copies the data you want to embed in the Word document into the Windows Clipboard.

❹ Click the Microsoft Word button on the taskbar.

This switches you back to Word.

❺ Position the insertion point on the blank line at the end of the memo, then open the Edit menu and choose Paste Special.

The Paste Special dialog box opens.

❻ Choose Microsoft Excel Worksheet Object in the As list box, then choose OK.

Excel embeds the worksheet object at the insertion point location. Do not choose the Paste **L**ink option button in the Paste Special dialog box. To embed the object, leave the **P**aste option button selected.

Now try editing the worksheet.

❼ Double-click the Excel worksheet object in the Word document.

The worksheet appears in its own Excel window within Word, as shown in Figure 7.8. You can use all the Excel functions, including the Chart toolbar, which appears when you select the chart. Now see what effect removing cleaning costs would have on your worksheet.

continues

To Work with Embedded Data (continued)

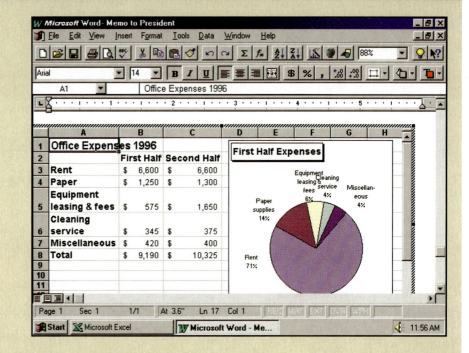

Figure 7.8
You can use Excel functions to edit embedded worksheet data in Word.

8 **Delete row 6 from the worksheet.**

This removes the cleaning service expenses from the worksheet. Notice that the total cell and the chart reflect the change in the data automatically.

9 **Click anywhere in the Word document outside the worksheet window.**

This closes the Excel worksheet, and displays the Word document, Memo To President. Notice that the change you made in the data appears in the Word worksheet object, as shown in Figure 7.9. Notice also that the chart reflects the latest information. If you switch back to Excel, however, you will see that no changes have been made to the original data.

Lesson 4: Working with Embedded Data

Figure 7.9
The changes appear in the embedded worksheet, but not in the original Excel file.

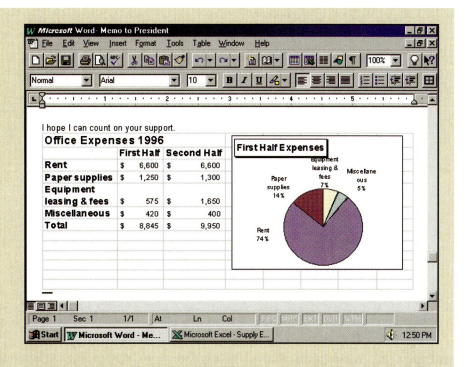

Save your work. If requested by your instructor, print two copies. Then close the document.

If you have completed your session on the computer, exit all open applications and Windows 95 before turning off the computer. Otherwise, continue with the "Applying Your Skills" case studies.

Project Summary

To	Do This
Switch applications	Click the button for the application you want to make active on the Windows 95 Taskbar.
Copy data between applications	Select the data to copy and click the Copy button on the Standard toolbar. Change to the target document, position the insertion point, and click the Paste button on the Standard toolbar.
Move data between applications	Select the data to move and click the Cut button on the Standard toolbar. Change to the target document, position the insertion point and click the Paste button on the Standard toolbar.
Link data between applications	Select the data to link and click the Copy button on the Standard toolbar. Change to the target document, position the insertion point and choose **E**dit, Paste **S**pecial. Click the Paste

continues

continued

To	Do This
	Link option button, select the object type, and choose OK.
Edit linked data	Double-click the data to open the source document. Make changes, then close the source document.
Embed data	Select the data to embed and click the Copy button on the Standard toolbar. Change to the target document, position the insertion point and choose **E**dit, Paste **S**pecial. Select the object type, and choose OK.
Edit embedding data	Double-click the data to open an editing window. Edit the document, then close the editing window.
Delete linked or embedded data	Click the data to select it and press Del.

Applying Your Skills

The following exercises enable you to practice the skills you have learned in this project. Take a few minutes to work through these exercises now.

Creating a Letter

A friend of yours is thinking about relocating to a new state and has asked you where your company has offices. You agree to provide a list of the states where your company has offices. You send her a letter that includes the list of sites you used in Project 5 to create a map.

To Create the Letter

1. In Excel, open the file Proj0703 and save it as **Relocate**.
2. In Word, open the file Proj0704 and save it as **Site Letter**.
3. Copy the entire list of offices and locations worksheet to the Clipboard.
4. Move to the end of the Site Letter in Word, and then paste the worksheet data.
5. Reformat the data if necessary.
6. Save the letter. If requested by your instructor, print two copies before closing the file.

Applying Your Skills

Adding Names to Your Club List

You write a memo to the Rollerblading club president regarding four people you think might be interested in joining the club. The president suggests adding their names to the phone list that you already created. Instead of retyping the names and phone numbers, you copy the data from the word processing document into Excel.

To Add the Names to Your List

1. Open the file Proj0705 in Excel, and save it as **Longer List**.
2. Open the file Proj0706 in Word for Windows, and save it as **New Names**.
3. Copy the table in the Word document to the Windows Clipboard.
4. Switch to Excel, and paste the data from the Clipboard to the end of the list.
5. Save the worksheet. If requested by your instructor, print two copies. Then close it.

Creating a Presentation for Potential Investors

You are heading into your second year in business and you want to give a presentation to potential investors that will convince them to provide capital for Sound Byte Music. You want to use this money to open a second store in a large shopping mall and to support your growing direct mail channel.

To do this effectively, you need to create a report in Word for Windows that includes narrative as well as a chart showing strong sales of CDs, cassette tapes, and books for the current year. Link a chart from an Excel worksheet to the presentation document in Word, then make some last minute changes in the Excel worksheet that will be updated in the linked chart.

To Create the Presentation

1. In Excel, open the file Proj0707 and save it as **Sound Byte Sales Data**.
2. In Word, open the file Proj0708 and save it as **Presentation To Investors**.
3. In the Sound Byte Sales Data worksheet, select the chart and copy it. Switch to Word and link the chart to the end of the Presentation to Investors document.
4. Switch back to the worksheet and make the following changes: in the 1st quarter Tape sales, change the value to **$15,000**; in the 3rd quarter Book sales, change the value to **$20,000**. Save the worksheet.
5. Switch back to the Word document to view the changes in the chart. Save the Presentation to Investors document. If requested by your instructor, print two copies. Then save and close all open documents.

Project 7   Using Excel with Other Programs

Comparing Regional Sales Figures

The New England Regional Sales Manager has submitted sales figures on a disk in a word processing document. You want to be able to compare the figures with other regional figures that you have already entered into Excel. Copy the data into the Excel worksheet, then use the data to create a chart comparing the two territories.

To Compare Regional Sales Figures

1. Open the file Proj0709 in Excel and save it as **New Sales**.
2. Open the file Proj0710 in Word for Windows and save it as **NE Sales**.
3. Copy the sales data from the Word document onto Sheet2 in the Excel workbook file.
4. Give Sheet2 a descriptive name, such as **NE**.
5. On Sheet3, reference the total sales for each of the two territories. Give Sheet3 a descriptive name, such as **Comparison**.
6. Create a chart on sheet3 comparing the total sales for the two territories.
7. Save the workbook file. If requested by your instructor, print two copies. Then close it.

Checking Your Skills

True/False

For each of the following, check T or F to indicate whether the statement is true or false.

__T __F   1. Use the Windows taskbar to switch among programs but not to open them.

__T __F   2. On the taskbar, click the Start button to start Microsoft Word.

__T __F   3. You cannot use the keyboard shortcuts for copying, cutting, and pasting, when you are integrating applications.

__T __F   4. If your system slows down, it could be because you have two copies of the same program open.

__T __F   5. Use the **E**dit, Paste **S**pecial command to link or embed data between applications.

Multiple Choice

Circle the letter of the correct answer for each of the following.

1. Which of the following is an easy way to switch among applications?

   a. press Ctrl+Del

   b. press Alt+Ctrl

c. click the application's button on the Windows taskbar

d. click the application's Start box

2. Which of the following can be passed over a link between applications?

   a. numbers
   b. charts
   c. ranges of cells
   d. all the above

3. When you _____ between two applications, one application opens within the other application.

   a. copy
   b. link
   c. move
   d. embed

4. Embedding and linking are part of a Windows feature called _____.

   a. OLE
   b. LEO
   c. ELO
   d. LLE

5. When you _____ data, you can make a change in the source and the destination automatically updates.

   a. link
   b. embed
   c. copy
   d. paste

Completion

In the blanks provided, write the correct answer for each of the following statements.

1. A link is a _____-way connection between the source worksheet and the client file.

2. If your system slows when embedding, you may want to consider sharing your data by _____ instead.

3. The _____ taskbar provides you with quick access to all the programs in the Microsoft Office suite of applications.

4. When pasting data into another program, the data locates at the _____ point.

5. The _____ application is the one in which the original object was created.

Working with Windows 95

Objectives

In this appendix, you learn how to
- Start Windows
- Use the Mouse
- Understand the Start Menu
- Identify the Elements of a Window
- "Manipulate Windows"
- Exit the Windows Program

Appendix A Working with Windows 95

Why Would I Do This?

Graphical user interface (GUI)
A computer application that uses pictures, graphics, menus, and commands to help users communicate with their computers.

Microsoft Windows 95 is a powerful operating environment that enables you to access the power of DOS without memorizing DOS commands and syntax. Windows 95 uses a *graphical user interface* (GUI) so that you can easily see on-screen the tools that you need to complete specific file and program management tasks.

This appendix, an overview of the Windows 95 environment, is designed to help you learn the basics of Windows 95.

Lesson 1: Starting Windows

Desktop
The background of the Windows screen, on which windows, icons, and dialog boxes appear.

The first thing you need to know about Windows is how to start the software. In this lesson, you learn how to start Windows; however, before you can start Windows, it must be installed on your computer. If you need to install Windows, refer to your Windows manual or ask your instructor for assistance.

Icon
A picture that represents an application, a file, or a system resource.

In most cases, Windows starts automatically when you turn on your computer. If your system is set up differently, you must start Windows from the DOS prompt (such as c:\>). Try starting the Windows program now.

To Start Windows

Shortcut
A shortcut gives you quick access to frequently used objects so you don't have to look through menus each time you need to use that object.

1. Turn on your computer and monitor.

   Most computers display technical information about the computer and the operating software installed on it.

   If Windows starts, you can skip step 2. Otherwise, you will see the DOS prompt c:\>.

2. At the DOS prompt, type **win** and then press ⏎Enter.

Taskbar
Contains the Start button, buttons for each open window and the current time.

   When you start the Windows program, a Microsoft Windows 95 banner displays for a few seconds; then the *desktop* appears (see Figure A.1).

Program *icons* that were created during installation (such as My Computer, Recycle Bin, and Network Neighborhood) are displayed on the desktop. Other icons may also appear, depending on how your system is set up. *Shortcuts* to frequently used objects (such as documents, printers, and network drives) can be placed on the desktop. The *taskbar* appears along the bottom edge of the desktop. The *Start button* appears at the left end of the taskbar.

Start button
A click of the Start button opens the Start menu.

Lesson 2: Using the Mouse

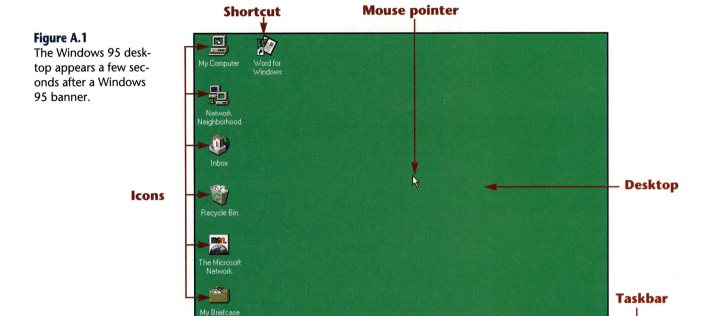

Figure A.1
The Windows 95 desktop appears a few seconds after a Windows 95 banner.

Lesson 2: Using the Mouse

Pull-down menus
Menus that cascade downward into the screen whenever you select a command from the menu bar.

Dialog box
A window that opens on-screen to provide information about the current action or to ask the user to provide additional information to complete the action.

Mouse
A pointing device used in many programs to make choices, select data, and otherwise communi-

Mouse pointer
A symbol that appears on-screen to indicate the current location of the mouse.

Mouse pad
A pad that provides a uniform surface for the mouse to slide on.

Windows is designed to be used with a *mouse*, so it's important that you learn how to use a mouse correctly. With a little practice, using a mouse is as easy as pointing to something with your finger. You can use the mouse to select icons, to make selections from *pull-down menus* and *dialog boxes*, and to select objects that you want to move or resize.

In the Windows desktop, you can use a mouse to

▶ Open windows

▶ Close windows

▶ Open menus

▶ Choose menu commands

▶ Rearrange on-screen items, such as icons and windows

The position of the mouse is indicated on-screen by a *mouse pointer*. Usually, the mouse pointer is an arrow, but it sometimes changes shape depending on the current action.

On-screen, the mouse pointer moves according to the movements of the mouse on your desk or on a *mouse pad*. To move the mouse pointer, simply move the mouse.

There are four basic mouse actions:

▶ *Click*. To point to an item, and then press and quickly release the left mouse button. You click to select an item, such as an option on a menu. To cancel a selection, click an empty area of the desktop. Unless otherwise specified, you use the left mouse button for all mouse actions.

Appendix A Working with Windows 95

> ► *Double-click.* To point to an item, and then press and release the left mouse button twice, as quickly as possible. You double-click to open or close windows and to start applications from icons.
>
> ► *Right-click.* To point to an item, and then press and release the right mouse button. This opens a Context menu, which gives you a shortcut to frequently used commands. To cancel a Context menu, click the left mouse button outside the menu.
>
> ► *Drag.* To point to an item, then press and hold down the left mouse button as you move the pointer to another location, and then release the mouse button. You drag to resize windows, move icons, and scroll.

If you have problems...

If you try to double-click but nothing happens, you may not be clicking fast enough. Try again.

Lesson 3: Understanding the Start Menu

The Start button on the taskbar gives you access to your applications, settings, recently opened documents, the Find utility, the **R**un command, the Help system, and the Sh**ut** Down command. Clicking the Start button opens the Start menu. Choosing the **P**rograms option at the top of the Start menu displays the **P**rograms menu, which lists the *program folders* on your system. Program folders are listed first, followed by shortcuts (see Figure A.2).

Program folder
Represented by an icon of a file folder with an application window in front of it, program folders contain shortcut icons and other program folders.

Figure A.2
Click the Start button to open the Start menu. All your programs are grouped together in the Programs menu.

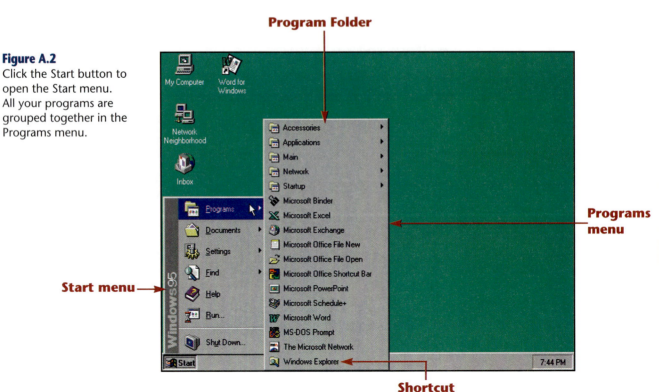

Lesson 4: Identifying the Elements of a Window

When the Start menu is open, moving the mouse pointer moves a selection bar through the menu options. When the selection bar highlights a menu command with a right-facing triangle, a submenu opens. Click the shortcut icon to start an application. If a menu command is followed by an ellipsis (...), clicking that command opens a dialog box.

Lesson 4: Identifying the Elements of a Window

In the Windows program, everything opens in a window. Applications, documents, and dialog boxes all open in windows. For example, double-clicking the My Computer icon opens the My Computer application into a window. Because window elements stay the same for all Windows applications, this section uses the My Computer window for illustration.

Title Bar

Across the top of each window is its title bar. A title bar contains the name of the open window as well as three buttons to manipulate windows. The Minimize button reduces windows to a button on the taskbar. The Maximize button expands windows to fill the desktop. The Close button closes the window.

Menu Bar

The menu bar gives you access to the application's menus. Menus enable you to select options that perform functions or carry out commands (see Figure A.3). The File menu in My Computer, for example, enables you to open, save, and print files.

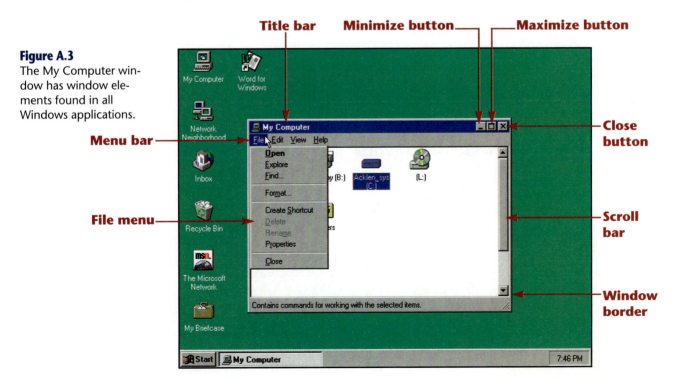

Figure A.3
The My Computer window has window elements found in all Windows applications.

Some menu options require you to enter additional information. When you select one of these options, a dialog box opens (see Figure A.4). You type the additional information, select from a list of options, or select a button. Most dialog boxes have a Cancel button, which closes the dialog box without saving the changes; an OK button, which closes the dialog box and saves the changes; and a Help button, which opens a Help window.

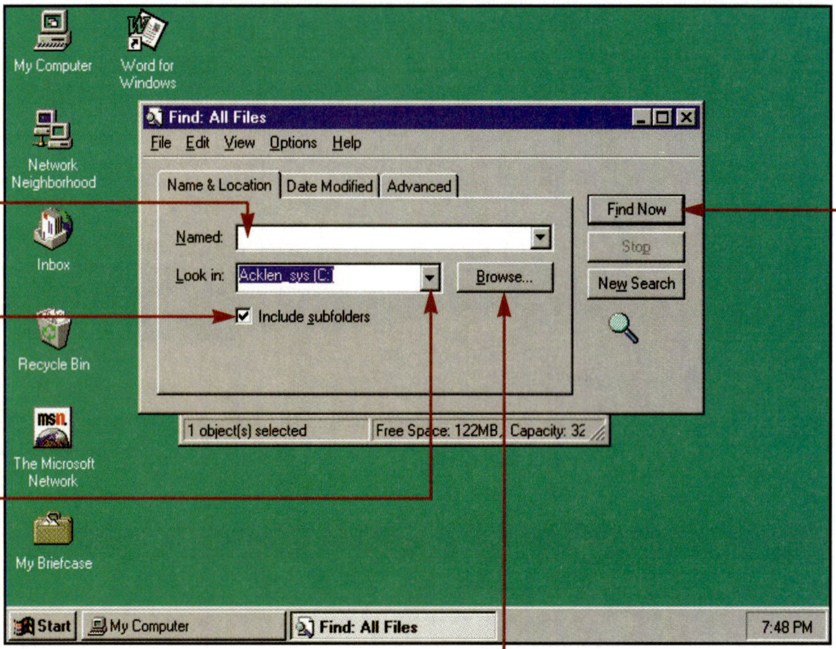

Figure A.4
You can use the options in the Find dialog box to search for a file.

Enter the name of the file here

Click here to select this option

Click here to select from a list

Click here to open a dialog box

Click here to find the file

Scroll Bar

Scroll bars appear when you have more information in a window than is currently displayed on-screen. A horizontal scroll bar appears along the bottom of a window and a vertical scroll bar appears along the right side of a window.

Window Bborder

The window border identifies the edge of the window. In most windows, it can be used to change the size of a window. The window corner is used to resize a window on two sides at the same time.

Lesson 5: Manipulating Windows

When you work with windows, you need to know how to arrange them. You can shrink the window into an icon or enlarge the window to fill the desktop. You can stack windows together or give them each an equal slice of the desktop.

Changing the size and position of a window enables you to see more than one application window, which makes copying and pasting data between

Lesson 5: Manipulating Windows

programs much easier. You can also move a window to any location on the desktop. By moving application windows, you can arrange your work on the Windows desktop just as you arrange papers on your desk.

Maximizing a Window

Maximize
To increase the size of a window so that it fills the entire screen.

You can *maximize* a window so that it fills the desktop. Maximizing a window gives you more space to work in. To maximize a window, click the Maximize button on the title bar.

Minimizing a Window

Minimize
To reduce a window to an icon.

When you *minimize* a window, it shrinks the window to an icon on the taskbar. Even though you can't see the window anymore, the application stays loaded in the computer's memory. To minimize a window, click the Minimize button on the title bar.

Restoring a Window

When a window is maximized, the Maximize button changes into a Restore button. Clicking the Restore button restores the window back to the original size and position before the window was maximized.

Closing a Window

When you are finished working in a window, you can close the window by clicking the Close button. Closing an application window exits the program, removing it from memory. When you click the Close button, the window (on the desktop) and the window button (on the taskbar) disappear.

Arranging Windows

Changing the size and position of a window enables you to see more than one application window, which makes copying and pasting data between programs much easier. You can also move a window to any location on the desktop. By moving application windows, you can arrange your work on the Windows desktop just as you arrange papers on your desk.

Tile
To arrange open windows on the desktop so that they do not overlap.

Cascade
To arrange open windows on the desktop so that they overlap, with only the title bar of each window (behind the top window) is dis-

Use one of the following options to arrange windows:

➤ Right-click the taskbar, and choose Tile **H**orizontally.

➤ Right-click the taskbar, and choose Tile **V**ertically. See Figure A.5 for an example.

➤ Right-click the taskbar, and choose **C**ascade. See Figure A.6 for an example.

➤ Click and drag the window's title bar to move the window around on the desktop.

➤ Click and drag a window border (or corner) to increase or decrease the size of the window.

Appendix A Working with Windows 95

Figure A.5
The windows are tiled vertically across the desktop.

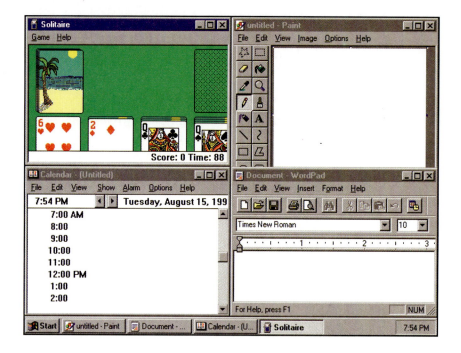

Figure A.6
The windows are cascaded on the desktop.

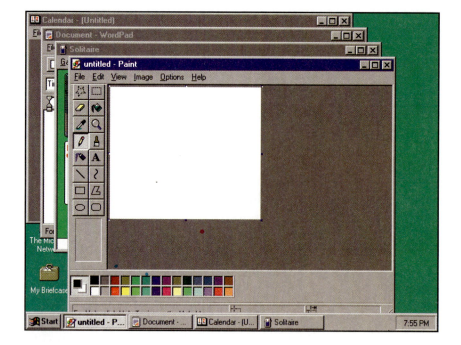

Lesson 6: Exiting the Windows Program

In Windows 95, you use the Sh**ut** Down command to exit the Windows program. You should always use this command, which closes all open applications and files, before you turn off the computer. If you haven't saved your work in an application when you choose this command, you'll be prompted to save your changes before Windows shuts down.

Lesson 6: Exiting the Windows Program

To Exit Windows

1. Click the Start button on the taskbar.
2. Choose Sh**u**t Down.
3. Choose **S**hut down the computer.
4. Choose **Y**es.

Windows displays a message asking you to wait while the computer is shutting down. When this process is complete, a message appears telling you that you can safely turn off your computer now.

INDEX

Symbols

3-D charts, 122
3-D Column button (Chart toolbar), 120
: (colons), 102
$ (dollar signs), 56
= (equal sign), 50-51
() (parentheses), 54

A

Absolute cell references (formulas), 56
active cells, 7-9
    navigating worksheets, 14-15
adding
    entries to dictionary, 80
    records to lists, 143-145
addresses (cells), 8-9
aligning data in cells, 67-68
Answer Wizard (Help function), 11, 13
applications
    copying data between, 163-164
    embedding data, 168-171
    linking data between, 165-168
    switching among, 160-163
area charts, 121
arguments (functions), 94, 97
ascending order (sorting records), 146
attributes, 64-66
AutoCalculate button, 7
AutoCalculate feature, 9, 54
AutoComplete feature, 41
AutoCorrect feature, 82
AutoFill command, 39-41
    copying formulas, 56
AutoFilter feature, 151-154
AutoFormat feature, 77-79
AutoSum button (Standard toolbar), 52-53, 95
AutoSum function, 52
AVERAGE function, 97-99
axes (charts), 114-115

B

bar charts, 121
Bold button (Formatting toolbar), 8
borders (cells), 74-77
buttons
    Chart toolbar
        3-D Column, 120
        Chart Type, 118
        Line Chart, 120
    Data Map toolbar
        Select Objects, 133
        Zoom In, 132
    Formatting toolbar
        Bold, 8
        Center, 67
        Center Across Columns, 68
        Currency Style, 72
    Formula bar
        Cancel, 17
        Enter, 17, 19, 50-52
    Print Preview toolbar, Print, 24, 128
    Standard toolbar
        AutoSum, 52-53, 95
        ChartWizard, 112
        Copy, 45, 55, 164
        Format Painter, 66
        Function Wizard, 93-94
        Help, 13
        Map, 129
        Open File, 34
        Paste, 45, 55, 164
        Print Preview, 24, 128
        Save, 21
        Spelling, 82
        Undo, 46
    taskbar
        Microsoft Excel, 163
        Microsoft Word, 164
        Start, 5, 24, 160, 178, 180-181, 185

C

Cancel button (formula bar), 17
cancelling menus, 8
cascading windows, 183-184
cell addresses, 8-9
cell contents, 9
    selecting, 38
CELL function, 97
cells, 8-9
    aligning data, 67-68
    AutoFill command, 39-41
    AutoFormat feature, 77-79
    borders, 74-77
    colors, 77
    copying
        data, 44-46
        formulas, 54-56
    dragging, 49
    entering data, 17
    errors, correcting, 18
    formatting numbers, 71-74
    formulas, 49-54
    moving data, 46-49
    ranges, 37
        naming, 88-90
        selecting, 37
    selecting, 37
    shading, 74-77
Cells command (Format menu), 64
Center Across Columns button (Formatting toolbar), 68
Center button (Formatting toolbar), 67
Chart toolbar
    3-D Column button, 120
    Chart Type button, 118
    Line Chart button, 120
Chart Type button (Chart toolbar), 118
Chart Type command (shortcut menu), 123
charts
    3-D, 122
    area, 121
    bar/column, 121
    colors, 124-125
    combination, 122
    creating, 112-115
    deleting, 126
    doughnut, 122
    embedded, 112
    formatting, 122-126
        text, 116-118

Charts

line, 118
moving, 126
pie, 118, 122
previewing, 128
printing, 126-129
radar, 122
resizing, 126
selecting types, 118-122
XY (scatter), 122

ChartWizard button (Standard toolbar), 112
Clear command (Edit menu), 46
clicking the mouse, 179
Clipboard, 44-46
Close button, 181, 183
closing
Help program, 13
windows, 183
worksheets, 24-25

colons (:), 102
colors, 77
charts, 124-125
column charts, 121
Column command (Format menu)
Column Width, 71
Standard Width, 71
column headings, 7, 9
Column Width command (shortcut menu), 78
columns
deleting, 41-43
inserting, 41-43
selecting, 8, 38
widths, changing, 69-71
Columns command (Insert menu), 42
combination charts, 122
commands
AutoFill, 39-41
Data menu
  Filter, 151, 154
  Form, 143, 149
  Sort, 146
Edit menu
  Clear, 46
  Copy, 44
  Cut, 46
  Delete, 42, 46
  Paste, 44
  Paste Special, 165, 169
  Undo, 40, 43, 46

File menu
  Exit, 24
  Open, 34
  Page Setup, 127
  Print, 22-23, 129, 134
  Print Preview, 24
  Save, 20
  Save As, 21, 36
Format menu
  AutoFormat, 78
  Cells, 64
  Column, 71
  Row, 71
Help menu
  Answer Wizard, 13
  Help Topics, 11
Insert menu
  Columns, 42
  Name, 88-89, 92, 141, 145
  Rows, 41-42
shortcut menu, 47
  Chart Type, 123
  Column Width, 78
  Copy, 54
  Delete, 48
  Edit Object, 122
  Format Cells, 73
  Format Data Series, 124
  Paste, 48, 54-55
Start menu
  Programs, 160, 180
  Shut Down, 24, 185
Tools menu
  AutoCorrect, 82
  Options, 41
  Spelling, 80
View menu
  Entire Map, 133
  Previous Map, 133
  Toolbars, 9, 118
computer crashes, 22
conditional statements, 102-105
Contents (Help function), 11
Copy button (Standard toolbar), 45, 55, 164
Copy command
Edit menu, 44
shortcut menu, 54
copying
data, 44-46
data between applications, 163-164
formulas, 54-56

crashes, 22
creating
charts, 112-115
lists, 140-142
maps, 129-134
worksheets, 16-19
Currency Style button (Formatting toolbar), 72
Current sheet tab, 7
current worksheets, 22
cursors, 17
Custom AutoFilter dialog box, 152-153
Cut command (Edit menu), 46

D

data
aligning in cells, 67-68
copying, 44-46
  between applications, 163-164
embedding in applications, 168-171
entering in worksheets, 16-19
linking between applications, 165-168
moving, 46-49
Data Form dialog box, 143-144, 149-150
data forms, 143
data labels (charts), 115
Data Map Control dialog boxes, 130-131
Data Map toolbar
Select Objects button, 133
Zoom In button, 132
Data menu commands
Filter
  AutoFilter, 151, 154
  Show All, 154
Form, 143, 149
Sort, 146
data series (charts), 113, 115
Databases, *see* **lists**
DATE function, 97
DDE (dynamic data exchange), 168
default settings, 4
Define Name dialog box, 89-92, 141-142, 145
Delete command
Edit menu, 42, 46
shortcut menu, 48

Formulas

deleting
  charts, 126
  named ranges, 92
  records, 149-150
  rows/columns, 41-43
descending order (sorting records), 146
deselecting ranges of cells, 40
Desktop, 178
dialog boxes, 179, 182
  AutoFormat, 78
  ChartWizard, 112-114
  Column Width, 78
  Custom AutoFilter, 152-153
  data form, 143-144, 149-150
  Data Map Control, 130-131
  Define Name, 89-90, 141-142, 145
  Defined Name, 92
  Delete, 43
  Edit Legend, 131-132
  Format Axis, 125
  Format Cells, 64-65, 68, 73-77
  Format Chart Title, 116-117
  Format Data Series, 124
  Function Wizard, 94
  Go To, 15
  Help Topics, 11
  Multiple Maps Available, 129
  Open, 34
  Page Setup, 127-128
  Paste Special, 165-166, 169
  Print, 22-23, 128-129
  Rename Sheet, 92
  Save As, 20-21, 36
  Shut Down Windows, 24-25
  Sort, 146-147
  Spelling, 80-82
  Toolbars, 9
dictionary, adding entries, 80
disabling AutoComplete feature, 41
dollar signs ($), 56
double-clicking the mouse, 180
doughnut charts, 122
dragging, 180
  ranges of cells, 49
Dynamic Data Exchange (DDE), 168

E

Edit Legend dialog box, 131-132
Edit menu commands
  Clear, 46
  Copy, 44
  Cut, 46
  Delete, 42, 46
  Paste, 44
  Paste Special, 165, 169
  Undo, 40, 43, 46
Edit Object command (shortcut menu), 122
embedded charts, 112
embedding, 168
  data in applications, 168-171
Enter button (Formula bar), 17, 19, 50-52
Entire Map command (View menu), 133
equal sign (=), 50-51
ERROR.TYPE function, 97
errors
  correcting in cells, 18
  formulas, 51
  functions, 95, 101
  linking data between applications, 168
  named ranges, 93
  sorting records, 148
EVEN function, 97
Excel
  exiting, 24-25
  screen elements, 7-10
  starting, 4-6
Exit command (File menu), 24
exiting
  Excel, 24-25
  Windows, 184-185

F

fields, 140-142
  sort fields, 145
File menu, 8, 181
File menu commands
  Exit, 24
  Open, 34
  Page Setup, 127
  Print, 22-23, 129, 134
  Print Preview, 24
  Save, 20
  Save As, 21, 36

files, 20
fill handles, 39
Filter command (Data menu)
  AutoFilter, 151, 154
  Show All, 154
filtering records, 151-154
Find (Help function), 11
floppy disks, 22
  saving worksheets, 20-21
fonts, 64-66
  formatting in charts, 117
footers/headers (charts), 127
Form command (Data menu), 143, 149
Format Axis dialog box, 125
Format Cells command (shortcut menu), 73
Format Chart Title dialog box, 116-117
Format Data Series command (shortcut menu), 124
Format menu commands
  AutoFormat, 78
  Cells, 64
  Column
    Column Width, 71
    Standard Width, 71
  Row, Row Height, 71
Format Painter button (Standard toolbar), 66
formatting, 14, 64
  AutoFormat feature, 77-79
  charts, 122-126
  disks, 21
  fonts/attributes, 64-66
  numbers in cells, 71-74
  text in charts, 116-118
Formatting toolbar, 7, 9, 66
  Bold button, 8
  Center Across Columns button, 68
  Center button, 67
  Currency Style button, 72
Formula bar, 7, 9
  Cancel button, 17
  Enter button, 17, 19, 50-52
  entering data, 17
  named ranges, navigating worksheets, 91-92
formulas, 16, 19, 49-54
  building via functions, 98-102
  compared to functions, 97
  copying, 54-56

Formulas

errors
    handling, 51
    messages, 101
precedence, 54
referencing worksheets, 92
Function Wizard button (Standard toolbar), 93-94
functions, 93-98
    Autocalculate, 9
    AutoSum, 52
    AVERAGE, 97-99
    building formulas, 98-102
    CELL, 97
    compared to formulas, 97
    conditional statements, 102-105
    DATE, 97
    error messages, 101
    ERROR.TYPE, 97
    EVEN, 97
    IF, 102-104
    MAX, 97
    MIN, 97
    NOW, 98
    ODD, 98
    PMT, 98
    PRODUCT, 98
    ROUND, 98
    selecting ranges, 97
    SUM, 93-96, 98
    TIME, 98
    TODAY, 93, 98

G-H

Go To dialog box, 15
Graphical User Interface (GUI), 178
hard disks, 22
    saving worksheets, 20
headers/footers (charts), 127
Help button (Standard toolbar), 13
Help menu commands
    Answer Wizard, 13
    Help Topics, 11
Help program, 10-13
    closing, 13
    printing, 13
Help Topics command (Help menu), 11

I

I-beam (mouse pointer), 17
icons, 178
IF function, 102-104
Index (Help function), 11
Insert menu commands
    Columns, 42
    Name, 88-89, 92
        Define, 141, 145
    Rows, 41-42
inserting rows/columns, 41, 43
integration, 160, 168

J-L

keyboard shortcuts, navigating worksheets, 16
legends
    charts, 114-115
    maps, 131-132
Line Chart button (Chart toolbar), 120
line charts, 118
linking data between applications, 165-168
lists, 140
    adding records, 143-145
    filtering records, 151-154
    naming, 140-142
    searching/deleting records, 149-150
    sorting records, 145-148
logical operators, 105

M

Map button (Standard toolbar), 129
maps
    creating, 129-134
    printing, 134
margins (charts), 127-128
Mathematical operators, 49
MAX function, 97
Maximize button, 181, 183
maximizing windows, 183
Menu bar, 7, 9, 181-182
menus
    cancelling, 8
    nested, 6
    pull-down menus, 179

Microsoft Excel button (taskbar), 163
Microsoft Office, 163
Microsoft Word button (taskbar), 164
Microsoft Word, *see* **Word**
MIN function, 97
Minimize button, 181-183
minimizing windows, 183
mouse, 179-180
    pad, 179
    pointer, 7-9, 17, 179
moving
    charts, 126
    data, 46-49
    see also navigating
Multiple Maps Available dialog box, 129
multiple rows/columns
    deleting, 43
    inserting, 43
multitasking, 160

N

Name box, 7-8, 10
Name command (Insert menu), 88-89, 92
    Define, 141, 145
named ranges
    deleting, 92
    error messages, 93
    navigating worksheets, 91-93
naming
    lists, 140-142
    ranges of cells, 88-90
    worksheets, 21, 92
navigating
    worksheets, 14-16, 91-93
    see also moving
nested menus, 6
nesting functions, 98
notes (charts), 115
NOW function, 98
numbers, formatting in cells, 71-74

O

Object Linking and Embedding (OLE), 168
objects, 115
ODD function, 98

OLE (Object Linking and Embedding), 168
on-line, 22
Open command (File menu), 34
Open File button (Standard toolbar), 34
opening worksheets, 34-36
operators (filtering records), 152-153
Options command (Tools menu), Edit tab, 41
orientation of text, 68

P

Page Setup command (File menu), 127
parentheses ( ), 54
Paste button (Standard toolbar), 45, 55, 164
Paste command
  Edit menu, 44
  shortcut menu, 48, 54-55
Paste Special command (Edit menu), 165, 169
pie charts, 118, 122
PMT function, 98
precedence (formulas), 54
previewing
  charts, 128
  worksheets, 23-24
Previous Map command (View menu), 133
Print button (Print Preview toolbar), 24, 128
Print command (File menu), 22-23, 129, 134
Print dialog box, 23
Print Preview button (Standard toolbar), 24, 128
Print Preview command (File menu), 24
Print Preview toolbar, 24, 128
printing
  charts, 126-129
  Help program, 13
  maps, 134
  worksheets, 22-24
PRODUCT function, 98
program folders, 180
Programs command (Start menu), 160, 180
Programs menu, 6
pull-down menus, 179

Q-R

radar charts, 122
Random access memory (RAM), 20-22
ranges, 37
  AutoFill command, 39-41
  deselecting, 40
  dragging, 49
  naming, 88-90
  selecting, 37
    for functions, 97
records, 140, 142
  adding to lists, 143-145
  deleting, 149-150
  filtering, 151-154
  search criteria, 149-150
  sorting, 145-148
referencing worksheets in formulas, 92
relative formulas, 55-56, 99, 102
Rename mode, 35
Rename Sheet dialog box, 92
resizing
  charts, 126
  windows, 183
Restore button, 183
restoring windows, 183
right-clicking the mouse, 180
ROUND function, 98
Row command (Format menu), Row Height, 71
row headings, 7, 10
rows
  deleting, 41, 43
  inserting, 41, 43
  selecting, 8, 38
Rows command (Insert menu), 41-42

S

Save As command (File menu), 21, 36
Save As dialog box, 20-21
Save button (toolbar), 21
Save command (File menu), 20
saving worksheets, 20-22
scatter charts, 122
screen elements (Excel), 7-10
ScreenTips, 13
scroll bars, 7, 10, 181-182
search criteria, records, 149-150

Select All button, 7, 10, 38
Select Objects button (Data Map toolbar), 133
selecting
  cells, 37-38
  chart types, 118-122
  columns, 8, 38
  ranges
    of cells, 37
    for functions, 97
  rows, 8, 38
  worksheets, 38
    entire, 38
    items, 37-38
servers, 168
shading cells, 74-77
Sheet tabs, 10
Shortcut menu commands, 47
  Chart Type, 123
  Column Width, 78
  Copy, 54
  Delete, 48
  Edit Object, 122
  Format Cells, 73
  Format Data Series, 124
  Paste, 48, 54-55
shortcuts, 178
Shut Down command (Start menu), 24, 185
Sort command (Data menu), 146
sort fields, 145
sorting records, 145-148
source files, 168
Spelling button (Standard toolbar), 82
Spelling Checker, 79-82
Spelling command (Tools menu), 80
Split box, 10
Split horizontal box, 7
Split vertical box, 7
Standard toolbar, 7, 10
  AutoSum button, 52-53, 95
  ChartWizard button, 112
  Copy button, 45, 55, 164
  Format Painter button, 66
  Function Wizard button, 93-94
  Help button, 13
  Map button, 129
  Open File button, 34
  Paste button, 45, 55, 164
  Print Preview button, 24, 128

Spelling button, 82
Undo button, 46
Start button (taskbar), 5, 24, 160, 178, 180-181, 185
Start menu commands
Programs, 160, 180
Shut Down, 24, 185
starting
Excel, 4-6
Windows, 178
status bar, 7, 10
SUM function, 93-96, 98
switching among applications, 160-163
syntax, 97

T

tables, 142
formats, 77-79
target files, 168
Taskbar, 178
Microsoft Excel button, 163
Microsoft Word button, 164
Start button, 5, 24, 160, 178, 180-181, 185
text, 16
correcting in cells, 18
formatting in charts, 116-118
orientation, 68
selecting, 38
wrapping, 68
tiling windows, 183-184
TIME function, 98
title bar, 7-8, 10, 181
titles (charts), 114-115
TODAY function, 93, 98
Toolbar, Save button, 21
Toolbars command (View menu), 9, 118
Tools menu commands
AutoCorrect, 82
Options, Edit tab, 41
Spelling, 80
ToolTips, 8

U-V

Undo button (Standard toolbar), 46
Undo command (Edit menu), 40, 43, 46

values, 16
View menu commands
Entire Map, 133
Previous Map, 133
Toolbars, 9, 118

W

widths, columns, 69-71
Windows
exiting, 184-185
mouse, 179-180
starting, 178
window elements, 181-182
windows
border, 181-182
cascading, 183-184
closing, 183
elements, 181-182
maximizing, 183
minimizing, 183
resizing, 183
restoring, 183
tiling, 183-184
wizards
Answer, 11, 13
Chart, 112
Function, 93-94
Word, 161-162
workbooks, 4, 10
Worksheets, 4
closing, 24-25
copying data, 44-46
entering data, 16-19
frames, 7-8, 10, 38
naming, 21, 92
navigating, 14-16, 91-93
opening, 34-36
previewing, 23-24
printing, 22-24
referencing in formulas, 92
saving, 20-22
selecting
entire, 38
items, 37-38
windows, 7, 10
wrapping text in cells, 68

X-Y-Z

x-axis (charts), 115
XLS file extension, 21
XY (scatter) charts, 122

y-axis (charts), 115

Zoom In button (Data Map toolbar), 132